T0328654

Cambridge Elements

Elements in the Philosophy of Physics
edited by
James Owen Weatherall
University of California, Irvine

FOUNDATIONS OF STATISTICAL MECHANICS

Roman Frigg
The London School of Economics and Political Science
Charlotte Werndl
University of Salzburg

CAMBRIDGE
UNIVERSITY PRESS

Shaftesbury Road, Cambridge CB2 8EA, United Kingdom

One Liberty Plaza, 20th Floor, New York, NY 10006, USA

477 Williamstown Road, Port Melbourne, VIC 3207, Australia

314–321, 3rd Floor, Plot 3, Splendor Forum, Jasola District Centre, New Delhi – 110025, India

103 Penang Road, #05–06/07, Visioncrest Commercial, Singapore 238467

Cambridge University Press is part of Cambridge University Press & Assessment, a department of the University of Cambridge.

We share the University's mission to contribute to society through the pursuit of education, learning and research at the highest international levels of excellence.

www.cambridge.org
Information on this title: www.cambridge.org/9781009468237

DOI: 10.1017/9781009022798

First published 2023

A catalogue record for this publication is available from the British Library.

ISBN 978-1-009-46823-7 Hardback
ISBN 978-1-009-01649-0 Paperback
ISSN 2632-413X (online)
ISSN 2632-4121 (print)

Foundations of Statistical Mechanics

Elements in the Philosophy of Physics

DOI: 10.1017/9781009022798
First published online: December 2023

Roman Frigg
The London School of Economics and Political Science

Charlotte Werndl
University of Salzburg

Author for correspondence: Charlotte Werndl, charlotte.werndl@sbg.ac.at

Abstract: Statistical mechanics is the third pillar of modern physics, next to quantum theory and relativity theory. It aims to account for the behaviour of macroscopic systems in terms of the dynamical laws that govern their microscopic constituents and probabilistic assumptions about them. In this Element, the authors investigate the philosophical and foundational issues that arise in SM. The authors introduce the two main theoretical approaches, Boltzmannian statistical mechanics and Gibbsian statistical mechanics, and discuss how they conceptualise equilibrium and explain the approach to it. In doing so, the authors examine how probabilities are introduced into the theories, how they deal with irreversibility, how they understand the relation between the micro and the macro level, and how the two approaches relate to each other. Throughout, the authors also pinpoint open problems that can be the subject of future research. This title is also available as Open Access on Cambridge Core.

Keywords: statistical mechanics, probability, equilibrium, Boltzmann, Gibbs

ISBNs: 9781009468237 (HB), 9781009016490 (PB), 9781009022798 (OC)
ISSNs: 2632-413X (online), 2632-4121 (print)

Contents

1 Introduction

1.1 The Aims of Statistical Mechanics

Statistical mechanics (SM) is the third pillar of modern physics, next to quantum theory and relativity theory. Its aim is to account for the behaviour of macroscopic systems in terms of the dynamical laws that govern their microscopic constituents and probabilistic assumptions about them. The use of probabilities is motivated by the fact that systems studied by SM have a large number of microscopic constituents. Paradigmatic examples of systems studied in SM are gases, liquids, crystals, and magnets, which all have a number of microscopic constituents that is of the order of Avogadro's number (6.022×10^{23}).[1]

The focal point of SM is a particular aspect of the behaviour of macrosystems, namely equilibrium. To introduce equilibrium, and to boost intuitions, let us consider a standard example. A gas is confined to the left half of a container with a dividing wall, as illustrated in Figure 1a. The gas is in *equilibrium* in the sense that there is no manifest change in any of its macro properties like pressure, temperature, and volume, and the gas will have these macro properties so long as the container remains unchanged. Now consider such a change: remove the dividing wall in the middle, as illustrated in Figure 1b. The gas is now no longer in equilibrium because it does not fill the container evenly. As a result, the gas starts spreading through the entire available volume, as illustrated in Figure 1c. The spreading of the gas comes to an end when the entire container is filled evenly and no further change takes place, as illustrated in Figure 1d. At this point, the gas has reached a new equilibrium. Since the process of spreading culminates in a new equilibrium, this process is an *approach to equilibrium*. A key characteristic of the approach to equilibrium is that it seems to be *irreversible*: systems move from non-equilibrium to equilibrium, but not vice versa: gases spread to fill the container evenly, but they do not spontaneously concentrate in the left half of the container. Since an irreversible approach to equilibrium is often associated with thermodynamics, this is referred to as *thermodynamic behaviour*.[2]

---

[1] From now on, we will use 'micro' and 'macro' as synonyms for 'microscopic' and 'macroscopic', and we will speak of macro systems and their micro constituents, as well as of macro or micro properties, macro or micro characterisations, and so on. We will also use 'micro-states' and 'macro-states', where we add the hyphen to indicate that they are unbreakable technical terms. We use 'SM systems' as a shorthand for 'the systems studied in SM'.

[2] This is commonly seen as a result of the second law of thermodynamics. However, as Brown and Uffink (2001) note, the irreversibility of the kind illustrated in our example is not part of the second law and has to be added as an independent principle to the theory, which they call the *minus-first law*.

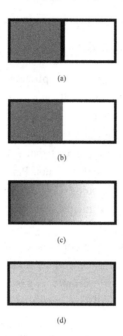

Figure 1 The spreading of gas when removing a shutter.

Characterising the state of equilibrium and accounting for why, and how, a system approaches equilibrium are the core tasks for SM. Sometimes these two problems are assigned to separate parts of SM, namely *equilibrium SM* and *non-equilibrium SM*.

What does characterising the state of equilibrium involve? We said that the gas is in equilibrium when there is no manifest change in any of its macro properties. This is a valid macro characterisation. Yet if the aim of SM is to account for the macro properties of a system in terms of the behaviour of its micro constituents, then we need a characterisation of equilibrium in micro-physical terms: what condition does the motion of the molecules in a gas have to satisfy for the gas to be in equilibrium? And how do the values of macroscopic properties like local pressure and local temperature depend on the state of motion of gas molecules? Equilibrium SM provides answers to these and related questions.

Turning to non-equilibrium, the core question is how the tendency of systems to move to equilibrium when prepared in a non-equilibrium state is grounded in the dynamics of the micro constituents of the system: what is it about the motions of molecules that leads them to spread so that the gas assumes a new equilibrium state when the shutter is removed? And, crucially, what accounts for the fact that the reverse process does not happen?

This Element focuses on these questions. This, however, is not to say that SM deals solely with equilibrium. While equilibrium occupies centre stage, SM also addresses other issues such as phase transitions, the entropy costs of computation, and the process of mixing substances; and in philosophical contexts SM has been employed to shed light on issues like the direction of time and the possibility of knowledge about the past. Space constraints prevent us from delving into these issues, and we will concentrate on equilibrium.

1.2 The Theoretical Landscape of SM

Foundational debates in many other areas of physics can take as their point of departure a generally accepted formalism and a clear understanding of what the theory is. A discussion of the nature of space and time, for instance, can base its considerations on the general theory of relativity, and a discussion of the foundations of quantum mechanics has the formalism of the theory as reference point. The situation in SM is different because, unlike quantum mechanics and relativity theory, SM has not yet found a generally accepted theoretical framework, let alone a canonical formulation. Those delving into SM find a multitude of different approaches and schools of thought, each with its own conceptual apparatus and formal structure.[3] A discussion of the foundations of SM can therefore not simply begin with a concise statement of the formalism of SM and its basic principles. Indeed, the choice, articulation, and justification of a theoretical framework for SM is an integral part of the foundational endeavour!

It has become customary in the foundations of SM to organise most (although not all) theoretical approaches in SM under one of two broad theoretical umbrellas. These umbrellas are known as Boltzmannian SM (BSM) and Gibbsian SM (GSM) because their core principles are attributed to Ludwig Boltzmann (1844–1906) and Josiah Willard Gibbs (1839–1903) respectively. Accordingly, approaches are then classified as 'Boltzmannian' or 'Gibbsian'.[4] In this Element, we follow this classificatory convention and use it to structure our discussion. We note, however, that from a historical point of view, this labelling is not entirely felicitous. While Boltzmann did indeed champion the approach now known as BSM, his work was in no way restricted to it.

---

[3] For reviews of these approaches see Frigg (2008b), Penrose (1970), Shenker (2017a, 2017b), Sklar (1993), and Uffink (2007).

[4] There is an interesting historical question about the origin and subsequent evolution of this schism. We cannot discuss this question here, but we speculate that it goes back to Ehrenfest and Ehrenfest-Afanassjewa's seminal review (1912/1959). While they do not use the labels BSM and GSM, they clearly separate a discussion of Boltzmann's ideas, which they discuss under the heading of 'The Modern Formulation of Statistico-Mechanical Investigations', and Gibbs' contributions, which they discuss in a section entitled 'W. Gibbs's *Elementary Principles in Statistical Mechanics*'.

Boltzmann in fact explored many different theoretical avenues, among them also ensemble methods that are now classified as Gibbsian. So 'BSM' is a neologism that should not be taken to be an accurate reflection of the scope of Boltzmann's own work.[5]

1.3 Outline

In this Element we discuss how BSM and GSM deal with the questions introduced in Section 1.1. Both BSM and GSM are formulated against the background of dynamical systems theory and probability theory. In Section 2 we introduce the basic concepts of both theories and state results that are important in the context of SM. In Section 3 we turn to BSM. We start by introducing the core concepts of BSM and then discuss different ways of developing them. Section 4 is dedicated to GSM. After introducing the formalism, we discuss its interpretation and different developments, and we end by considering the relation between BSM and GSM.

It goes without saying that omissions are inevitable. Some of them we have already announced in Section 1.1: we focus on equilibrium and the approach to it, and we set aside topics like phase transitions and the entropy costs of computation, and we will only briefly touch on questions concerning reductionism.[6] In addition to these, we set aside approaches to SM that do not clearly fall under the umbrella of either BSM or GSM, which implies that we do not discuss the Boltzmann equation.[7]

2 Mechanics and Probability

As the name 'statistical mechanics' indicates, SM aims to give an account of the behaviour of systems in terms of mechanics and statistics. The use of the word 'statistics' in this context is, however, out of sync with its modern use, where the term usually means something like 'the technology of extracting meaning from data' (Hand 2008, 1). As a branch of theoretical physics, SM is not concerned with the collection and interpretation of data (although data are of course important in testing the theory). In the second half of the nineteenth century, when the foundations of the discipline were laid, one of the main uses of the term 'statistics' was also to designate a 'description of the properties or behaviour of a collection of many atoms, molecules, and so on, based on the application of probability theory' (*OED* 'statistics'). So a 'statistical' treatment of

---

[5] For an overview of Boltzmann's contributions to SM see Uffink (2022); for detailed discussions see, for instance, Brush (1976), Cercignani (1998), Darrigol (2018), and Uffink (2007).

[6] For recent discussions of reduction with special focus on statistical mechanics, see Batterman (2002), Butterfield (2011a, 2011b), Lavis, Kühn, and Frigg (2021), and Palacios (2022).

[7] For a discussion of the Boltzmann equation, see Uffink (2007).

a problem is simply a treatment in terms of probability theory. This use of 'statistics' has become less common, and hence 'probabilistic mechanics' might better describe the discipline to a modern reader. But, for better or worse, historical labels stick. What this short excursion into the etymology of 'statistical mechanics' brings home is that the theory builds on two other disciplines, namely mechanics and probability, which provide its background theories.

The aim of this section is to introduce these background theories. The mechanical background theory against which SM is formulated can be either classical mechanics or quantum mechanics, resulting in either classical SM or quantum SM. Foundational debates are by and large conducted in the context of classical SM. We follow this practice in this Element, and for this reason the current section focuses on classical mechanics.[8]

The section is structured as follows. We begin by introducing dynamical systems at a general level, along with some basic mechanical notions like *trajectory*, *measure*, and *determinism* (Section 2.1). We then have a closer look at a specific class of dynamical systems, Hamiltonian systems, which are important in this context because they provide the fundamental structure of SM systems (Section 2.2). Hamiltonian systems have two dynamical properties that feature prominently in discussions about SM, namely time-reversal invariance (Section 2.3) and Poincaré recurrence (Section 2.4). Being ergodic is a property that certain time evolutions possess. This property plays an important role in SM because different approaches appeal to it to justify the equilibrium behaviour of SM systems (Section 2.5). This brings our discussion of mechanics to a conclusion, and we turn to probability. We introduce the basic formalism of probability theory and discuss the three main philosophical interpretations of probability (Section 2.6).

2.1 Dynamical Systems

At the level of their micro constituents, SM systems have the structure of a so-called *dynamical system*, a triple (X, ϕ_t, μ).[9] This is illustrated in Figure 2. Here, X is the *state space* of the system: it contains all states that, the system could possibly assume. In classical mechanics, the state of motion of an object (understood as a point particle) is completely specified by saying what its position and momentum are. If a system consists of several objects, the state of motion of the system is specified by saying what the positions and the momenta of all its objects are. Molecules move in three-dimensional physical space, and so a molecule has

---

[8] For a discussion of foundational issues in quantum SM see, for instance, Emch (2007).
[9] Our characterisation of a dynamical system is intuitive. For mathematical discussions see, for instance, Arnold and Avez (1968) and Katok and Hasselblatt (1995).

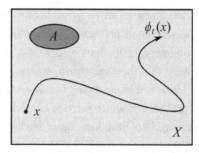

Figure 2 A dynamical system and a subset $A \subseteq X$.

three degrees of freedom. This means that a specification of the position of the molecule requires three parameters, one for each spatial direction. Since the molecule has a momentum in each direction, a further three parameters are needed to specify its momentum. So we need six parameters to specify the state of motion of a molecule. Accordingly, the specification of the state of the entire gas with n molecules requires $6n$ parameters. Hence, X is a $6n$-dimensional space containing the positions and momenta of all molecules.

The second element of a dynamical system, ϕ_t, is the *time evolution function*. This function specifies how the state of a system changes over time, and we write $\phi_t(x)$ to denote the state into which an initial state x evolves after time t. If the time evolution is specified by equations of motion like Newton's, Lagrange's, or Hamilton's, then $\phi_t(x)$ is the solution of that equation (we discuss Hamilton's equations in more detail in the next section). As time passes, $\phi_t(x)$ draws a 'line' through X that represents the time evolution of a system that was initially in state x; this 'line' is called a *trajectory*. This is illustrated in Figure 1.

The third element of a dynamical system, μ, is a *measure* on X. At a general level, a measure is a device to attribute a size to an object. Familiar examples are the attribution of a length to a segment of a line, a surface to a part of a plane, and a volume to a portion of space. From a mathematical point of view X is a set, and the measure μ attributes a 'size' – or 'measure' – to subsets of X in much the same way in which a ruler attributes a length to, say, a pencil. If the measure μ is able to attribute a size to a particular subset $A \subseteq X$, then A is said to be *measurable*. In what follows we assume that all sets are measurable. If a measure is such that $\mu(X) = 1$, then the measure is *normalised*.

Things can be measured in different ways. One measure is of particular importance in the current context: the so-called *uniform Lebesgue measure*. This measure is a mathematically precise rendering of the measure we use when attributing lengths and surfaces to objects. For instance, the interval [2, 5] has uniform Lebesgue measure (or length) 3, and a circle with radius r has uniform Lebesgue measure (or surface) of πr^2.

The time evolution ϕ_t is deterministic. It is common to define determinism in terms of possible worlds (Earman 1986, 13). Let W be the class of all physically possible worlds. The world $w \in W$ is deterministic if and only if for *any* world $w' \in W$ it is the case that: if w and w' are in the same state at some time t_0, then they are in the same state at *all* times t. This definition can be restricted to an isolated subsystem s of w. Consider the subset world $W_s \subseteq W$ of all possible worlds which contain an isolated counterpart of s, and let s' be the isolated counterpart of s in w'. Then s is deterministic if and only if for *any* world $w' \in W_s$ it is the case that if s and s' are in the same state at some time t_0, then they are in the same state at *all* times t. The system s can be a dynamical system of the kind we have just introduced. Determinism then implies that every state x has exactly one past and exactly one future, or, in geometrical terms, trajectories cannot intersect (neither themselves nor other trajectories).

2.2 Hamiltonian Mechanics

The notion of a dynamical system introduced in the previous section is extremely general, and more structure must be added to make it useful for the treatment of SM systems. The structure that is usually added is that of Hamiltonian mechanics.[10]

In Hamiltonian mechanics, the state of an object is described by its position q and its momentum p. In fact, there is a q-and-p pair for every degree of freedom. Hence, for a gas with n molecules moving in the three-dimensional physical space there are $3n$ q-and-p pairs. The $3n$ pairs constitute the state space X of the system, which in this context is often referred to as *phase space* (and since having $3n$ pairs means having $6n$ variables, the phase space has $6n$ dimensions as noted previously).

The Hamiltonian equations of motion are

$$\dot{q}_k = \frac{\partial H}{\partial p_k} \text{ and } \dot{p}_k = -\frac{\partial H}{\partial q_k},$$

where the dot indicates a derivative with respect to time and the index k ranges over all degrees of freedom (so, for a gas we have $k = 1, \ldots, 3n$). This defines a system of k differential equations, and the solution to this equation is the time evolution function ϕ_t of the system. Solving these equations for SM systems is usually a practical impossibility, and so we will not be able to write down ϕ_t explicitly. This does not render Hamiltonian mechanics useless. In fact, the equations ensure that ϕ_t has a number of general features, and these can be

---

[10] For a brief introduction see, for instance, Argyris, Faust, and Haase (1994, ch. 4).

established even if ϕ_t is not explicitly known. In the remainder of this section we review some of the features that are central to SM.

The Hamiltonian equations contain the function H, which is called the *Hamiltonian* of the system. The Hamiltonian H is the energy function of the system, which, in general, depends on all coordinates q_k and p_k. So, the Hamiltonian equations of motion specify how a system evolves in time based on the energy function of the system. If the energy of the system does not explicitly depend on time (which is the case, for instance, if a system is not driven by outside influences like pushes or kicks), then the system is *autonomous*. In an autonomous system, H is a conserved quantity (or a 'constant of motion'), meaning that it does not change over the course of time. This has the immediate consequence that any function $f(H)$ is a conserved quantity too.

The gas that we used as our introductory example is an autonomous system: it is isolated from the environment through the box and once the shutter has been removed, it is not subject to any outside disturbances. The gas is no exception, and typical systems in SM are autonomous Hamiltonian systems. The fact that the energy is conserved has an important consequence. Once the energy of the system is fixed to have a certain value E, the conservation of energy means that $H = E$ must hold all the time. H is a function of the coordinates q_k and p_k, which means that it defines a hypersurface X_E in X. This surface has one dimension fewer than X itself. In the case of the gas, it is therefore $6n - 1$ dimensional. This surface is known as the *energy hypersurface*.[11] Since $H = E$ holds at all times, it follows that the motion of the system is confined to the energy hypersurface: trajectories that start in an initial condition x in the energy hypersurface will never leave the hypersurface.

The total energy of the system may not be the only conserved quantity. Depending on the nature of the system, other quantities may be conserved too. From a formal point of view, each conserved quantity is a function Q of the coordinates q_k and p_k for which $Q = C$ holds for all times, where C is the value that Q assumes. In geometric terms, each conserved quantity defines a hypersurface to which trajectories remain confined. Such surfaces are also called *invariant hypersurfaces*. The crucial aspect (and this will be important later on) is that these hypersurfaces divide the phase space into regions that are 'disconnected' in the sense that trajectories cannot penetrate the surface to get to the other side. This is schematically illustrated in Figure 3, where we see an invariant surface and three trajectories. While Trajectory 1 and Trajectory 2 are

---

[11] It is a *hyper*surface because 'surface' has the connotation of being two-dimensional, like a tabletop, which the surface of constant energy is not.

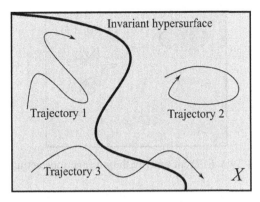

Figure 3 Invariant surface.

possible, Trajectory 3 is impossible because no trajectory can cross an invariant hypersurface. So, invariant hypersurfaces divide the state space X into sectors that are mapped onto themselves under the dynamics.

Autonomous Hamiltonian systems have an important feature that is related to the third element of a dynamical system, the measure μ. As we have seen in the previous section, a measure allows us to attribute a 'size' or 'measure' to a part of the state space such as the blob A shown in Figure 2. A blob ultimately consists of points and, as we have seen, points lie on trajectories: a point x evolves into $\phi_t(x)$ as time evolves. This means that the evolution of the blob as whole is determined by the evolution of its constituent points. We write $\phi_t(A)$ to denote the time-evolved blob. We can now ask *how* a blob evolves. One of the most important questions to ask about the evolution of blobs is what happens to their measure. The initial measure of the blob is $\mu(A)$, and the measure of the time-evolved blob is $\mu(\phi_t(A))$. How do these compare? If these two are identical – namely $\mu(A) = \mu(\phi_t(A))$ – for all blobs $A \subseteq X$ and all times t, then ϕ_t is *measure preserving*. An important result in Hamiltonian mechanics, known as *Liouville's theorem*, says that any ϕ_t that is the solution of the Hamiltonian equations of motion is measure preserving. This means that if a system is governed by the Hamiltonian equations, a blob can change its shape but not its size. This is illustrated in Figure 4, which shows how A evolves under two different time evolution functions, $\phi_t^{(1)}$ and $\phi_t^{(2)}$. Under the first function, A evolves into $\phi_t^{(1)}(A)$, which does not have the same shape as A but is of the same size. This kind of evolution is allowed under the Hamiltonian equations of motion. Under the second function, A evolves into $\phi_t^{(2)}(A)$, which is smaller than A. This is ruled out by the Hamiltonian equations, and a function like $\phi_t^{(2)}$ could not be a solution of the equations. It is important to point out that this feature is specific to the Hamiltonian equations. Far from ruled out in general,

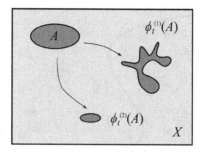

Figure 4 Two different time evolution functions acting on A.

evolutions like $\phi_t^{(2)}$ are common in other contexts, and they are allowed, for instance, if the guiding equation is Newton's rather than Hamilton's.

Before moving on, we briefly note that even though Hamiltonian mechanics is assumed to be the fundamental theory of SM systems, in practical calculations other dynamical laws are sometimes considered. Typical examples are the Kac ring or the baker's gas.[12] These dynamical laws are typically chosen for two reasons: they are simple and can be implemented relatively easily on computers, and yet they share important features with the full Hamiltonian dynamics, most notably measure preservation. So, even when considerations are made with alternative dynamical laws, Hamiltonian mechanics informs and guides the choice.

2.3 Time-Reversal Invariance

An important aspect of Hamiltonian dynamics is time-reversal invariance.[13] To introduce the concept, imagine you are watching a movie showing a ball moving horizontally from the left to the right. Intuitively, reversing the time of the process amounts to playing the movie backward, which results in you seeing a ball moving horizontally from the right to the left. Assume now that the moving balls are governed by a theory T, which regulates which processes are allowed and which are banned. Theory T is time-reversal invariant if and only if for *every* process that is allowed by the theory, its time reverse is allowed too.[14]

To give a precise statement of this idea, we need two things. The first is a time-reversal transformation $t \rightarrow - t$. The second is the reversal of an instantaneous state of a system. Consider again our ball. Its state is given by the

---

[12] For a discussion of the Kac ring, see Jebeile (2020); for the baker's gas, see Lavis (2008).

[13] In what follows we restrict attention to autonomous Hamiltonian systems.

[14] Note that time-reversal invariance does *not* imply that processes must be such that they look the same in both temporal directions: processes do not have to be palindromic. In our example, you see a ball moving from left to right in one temporal direction and from right to left in the other. For detailed discussions of time-reversal invariance see, for instance, Roberts (2022) and Uffink (2001).

coordinates q and p. When we stop the movie and start playing it backwards, the position of the ball remains unchanged, but its momentum flips from p to $-p$. So, the time-reversed state of $(q,\ p)$ is $(q, -p)$. Hence, performing a so-called time-reversal transformation amounts to replacing t by $-t$ and p by $-p$.

In Hamiltonian mechanics the verdict on whether a process is allowed is cast by the Hamiltonian equations of motion: if a process satisfies the equations, it is allowed, and if not, it is ruled out. So, let us see how the Hamiltonian equations behave under a time-reversal transformation. Some elementary algebraic manipulations show that the equations are left unchanged if you replace t by $-t$ and p by $-p$. This means that processes unfolding backward in time are governed by the same equation as those unfolding forward in time, and this means that the theory – the Hamiltonian equations – cast the same verdict about what is allowed in both directions of time. Hence, Hamiltonian mechanics is time-reversal invariant. This means that if a process from an initial state $(q_i,\ p_i)$ to a final state $(q_f,\ p_f)$ during timespan Δt is allowed, then a process starting in state $(q_f, -p_f)$ and ending in $(q_i, -p_i)$ during timespan Δt is allowed too. As we will see, this is the crucial formal ingredient of what is now known as Loschmidt's reversibility objection.

2.4 Poincaré Recurrence

How do Hamiltonian systems behave in the long run? With an eye on irreversibility, one might hope that SM systems will be such that they start in one part of X and then end up in another part of X. Poincaré's so-called *recurrence theorem* establishes that this cannot be. Consider a system with a state space of finite measure ($\mu(X) < \infty$) and with a dynamics that is measure preserving and maps the state space onto itself ($\phi_t(X) = X$ for all t). The theorem then says that for any set $A \subseteq X$ of finite measure ($\mu(A) > 0$) it is the case that almost every point x in A will return to A infinitely many times as $t \rightarrow \infty$. The set A can be chosen to be an arbitrarily small area around an initial condition x. The theorem then says that for almost all initial conditions, the system will return arbitrarily close to the initial condition infinitely many times. The time that it takes the system to return close to its initial condition is called the *recurrence time*.[15]

The Hamiltonian systems that are of interest in SM satisfy the requirements of the theorem: they are measure preserving (as we have seen), and since they have finite energy and are bounded in space (they are things like vessels full of gas), the accessible region of the state space is bounded. We can then 'throw away' the regions of the state space that the system cannot access and associate X with the accessible region, which is finite. Hence, SM systems show Poincaré

---

[15] For a discussion of Poincaré recurrence, see, for instance, Cornfeld, Fomin, and Sinai (1982).

recurrence. As we will see, this is the mathematical backbone of what is now known as Zermelo's recurrence objection.

2.5 Ergodicity

Among the many properties that a time evolution can have, ergodicity is of particular importance because it plays a crucial role in discussions of both BSM and GSM.[16] Consider a function $f : X \to \mathbb{C}$, where '$\mathbb{C}$' denotes the complex numbers. Sometimes such a function is called a 'phase function' because in the context of Hamiltonian mechanics X is also referred to as the phase space (Section 2.2). The *space average $\bar{f}$* of f (sometimes also called 'phase average', for the same reasons) is

$$\bar{f} = \int_X f \, dx. \tag{1}$$

The *time average of the same function is*

$$f^*(x) = \lim_{\tau \to \infty} \int_{t_0}^{t_0 + \tau} f(\phi_t(x)) dt, \tag{2}$$

where x is the initial condition of the trajectory at the initial time t_0. It is important to note that the time average depends on the initial condition and can, in principle, be different for different initial conditions. Intuitively, the space average gives us information about the mean distribution over space. If, for instance, a village occupies an area of 3 square kilometres, and there are 100, 300, and 800 dwellers in the first, second, and third square kilometre respectively, then the average population per square kilometre is 400. The time average gives us information about the distribution over time. Consider the first square kilometre of our village and trace its population over time. You find that it had 50 dwellers from 1800 to 1900 and 100 dwellers from 1900 to 2000. The time average of the population in the first square kilometre over the period from 1800 to 2000 is then 75.

The so-called *Birkhoff theorem* states that $f^*(x)$ exists for almost all initial conditions and does not depend on t_0 (but may well depend on x). The qualification 'almost all' means all except, perhaps, for a set of measure zero. Intuitively, measure zero sets are small: a point in an interval has measure zero, and so does a line within a plane. With this result in the background, we can state the definition of ergodicity: a dynamical system is ergodic if and only if

---

[16] For rigorous discussions of ergodicity and ergodic theory, see, for instance, Arnold and Avez (1968), Cornfeld, Fomin, and Sinai (1982), and Petersen (1983).

$f^*(x) = \bar{f}$ for almost all x. As we will see, ergodicity is a non-trivial property and many systems – also Hamiltonian systems – are not ergodic.

Without loss of generality, we now assume that the measure is *normalised*, that is: $\mu(X) = 1$.[17] Two consequences of ergodicity are worth emphasising because both play central roles in SM. The first consequence transpires if we choose f to be the so-called *characteristic function* of a set A in X: the function assumes value one for x that are in A and zero for x outside A. The space average for this function is then simply the measure of A, and the time average is the fraction of time that the system spends in A in the long run. If the system is ergodic, it follows that for any area A in X, the fraction of time the system spends in A is equal to the measure of A. This is illustrated in Figure 5. If, for instance, A takes up a quarter of X, then the system will spend a quarter of its time in A in the long run, and this is the case for almost all initial conditions.

The second consequence is that since the preceding holds for any A in X, there cannot be a part B of the state space (with $\mu(B) > 0$) that the system does not visit. As we have seen in Section 2.2, if a system has invariant hypersurfaces, these divide the state space into disconnected areas. This is incompatible with ergodicity, and so it follows immediately that an ergodic system must not have invariant hypersurfaces. This is sometimes expressed by saying that ergodic systems are 'indecomposable' or 'metrically transitive'.

An important question concerns the space on which a system is ergodic. So far we have formulated everything in terms of X, the state space of the system. This is a choice of convenience. As we have seen, an autonomous Hamiltonian system always has at least one conserved quantity, namely the energy of the system, and so its motion is always confined to the energy hypersurface X_E.

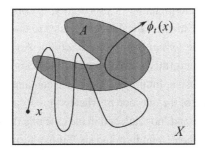

Figure 5 Ergodicity.

---

[17] We can do this without loss of generality because, as we have seen, SM systems have a finite phase space and one can then always choose the measure so that the entire space has measure one.

Hence, a Hamiltonian system cannot possibly be ergodic on X. This, however, does not preclude it from potentially being ergodic on X_E, or, indeed, a subspace of X_E. Crucial discussions in SM revolve around exactly this issue: whether the system is ergodic on X_E or a relevant subspace of it.

As noted, many systems are not ergodic, not even when restricting consideration to the energy hypersurface X_E. But now there is a surprising result. An *ergodic decomposition* of a system is a partition of the state space into different parts so that the parts are invariant under the dynamics (i.e. are mapped onto themselves under ϕ_t) and that, for all parts (of which there can be a finite or an infinite number), the dynamics within the part is ergodic. The *ergodic decomposition theorem* makes the – intuitively surprising – statement that such a decomposition exists for *every* measure-preserving dynamical system with a normalised measure, and that the decomposition is unique. In other words, the dynamics of a system can be as complex as we like and the interactions between the constituents of the system can be as strong and intricate as we like, and yet there exists a unique ergodic decomposition of the state space of the system. We will come back to this result later in the Element.

2.6 Probability Theory

Probability is a familiar concept. We consider the probability of rain before going out, or we consider the probability of getting the number three when throwing a die. As we will see, in the context of SM we are interested in the probability of a system approaching equilibrium, the probability of entropy increasing, and the probability of finding the system in a certain state. The theory of probability can be divided into two parts. The first part, the formal theory of probability, develops the mathematical apparatus of probability. The second part, the interpretation of probability, is concerned with how the formal apparatus of the mathematical theory relates to the real world.

Let us begin with the *formal theory of probability*. An *event space* Ω is the space of all possible events (this is also known as the *outcome space*). The events in Ω are mutually exclusive. Intuitively, this space contains all basic events that can happen. In the case of the question of whether it will rain, the space contains the two elements, 'rain' and 'no rain', and in the case of a die it has six elements, the numbers one, two, three, four, five, and six. From a formal point of view Ω is a set, and so the event space for the die is the set $\{1, 2, 3, 4, 5, 6\}$. But we may not only be interested in basic events. When throwing a die, for instance, we may not only be interested in getting, say, the number three, but also in events like getting an even number or getting a number smaller than four. Such events are associated with subsets of Ω: getting an even number is associated with the subset $\{2, 4, 6\}$

and getting a number smaller than four with $\{1, 2, 3\}$. We can now also form a set of subsets. For instance, we can construct the set consisting of the sets $\{2, 4, 6\}$ and $\{1, 2\}$: $\{\{2, 4, 6\}, \{1, 2\}\}$. Let Σ be a set of subsets of Ω. The set Σ is a *sigma-algebra* if and only if it satisfies the following conditions: Ω is an element of Σ; if s is an element of Σ, then also $\Omega\backslash s$ is element of Σ (where '$\Omega\backslash s$' denotes the complement of s with respect to Ω); and every countable union of subsets of Ω is in Σ. A *probability measure* then is a function $p: \Sigma \to [0, 1]$ such that $p(\Omega) = 1$ and $p(s_1 \cup s_2) = p(s_1) + p(s_2)$ for all mutually exclusive events s_1 and s_2 in Σ, where '$\cup$' denotes the set union. Or, more intuitively, a probability measure is a function that assigns every event (basic and non-basic) a number between zero and one, and this number then is the probability of the event.[18] The triple (Ω, Σ, p) is called a *probability space*. The probability of s_1 conditional on s_2 is $p(s_1|s_2) = p(s_1 \cap s_2)/p(s_2)$ provided that $p(s_2) > 0$, where '$\cap$' denotes the set intersection.

The probability space of a die is relatively simple. Not all probability spaces are like this. Some situations are such that the event space is continuous. As an example, consider a dartboard. In principle, a dart can hit any point of the dartboard. So, the event space is the entire disk that constitutes the dartboard, which has an uncountable infinity of points. In such cases, the probability measure is defined by a normalised function ρ on the event space via the following equation:

$$p(R) = \int_R \rho \, d\omega, \tag{3}$$

where R is a subset of Ω. The function ρ is called a *probability density*. The condition that ρ be normalised means that

$$\int_\Omega \rho \, d\omega = 1. \tag{4}$$

In effect this is just the 'continuous version' of the condition that probabilities add up to one.

Let us now very briefly turn to the second part, the interpretation of probability.[19] An interpretation of probability specifies the meaning of probability statements. Interpretations of probability fall into two groups: objective

---

[18] These conditions are known as the *axioms of probability*. What we have presented here is the standard axiomatisation of probability. There are alternative axiomatisations. Nothing in what follows depends on which axioms we choose. For a discussion of alternative axiomatisations, see Lyon (2016). For an in-depth discussion of the formal theory of probability, see, for instance, Fine (1973).

[19] We here largely follow Hájek's (2019) classification of interpretations but concentrate on accounts that are, at least in principle, candidates for the interpretation of SM probabilities.

and subjective. Objective interpretations take probabilistic statements to describe objective features of the world. If, say, the probability of obtaining number three when throwing a die is said to be 1/6, then an objectivist sees this as being a statement of fact. Subjectivists, by contrast, see probabilities as *credences*. A credence is a degree of belief that an agent has (or ought to have) in the occurrence of a certain event.

The foremost question for the objectivist is: what facts in the world do probabilities describe? The two most common answers to this question are relative frequencies and propensities. *Frequentism* interprets probabilities as frequencies that are calculated in a sequence of events of the same kind. Frequencies thereby provide a statistical summary of the distribution of certain features in that sequence. For a frequentist, the statement that the probability for number three is 1/6 simply means that in a sequence of throws of a die, number three has come up in 1/6th of the cases. Frequentism comes in different versions, the most important division being between finite and infinite frequentism. Infinite frequentism, most prominently developed by von Mises, interprets probabilities as limiting relative frequencies of events in sequences extended to infinity. Finite frequentism insists that in the real world we never have infinite sequences of events and hence interprets probabilities in terms of relative frequencies in finite sequences. One of the main problems of finite frequentism is that one cannot rule out that one gets an 'atypical' sequence of events (you *may* get the number three a hundred times in a series of a hundred throws). So-called *Humean best systems* accounts address this problem by requiring that probabilities are not determined by finite frequencies alone; they also have to be consequences of a system of laws that strikes the best balance between the theoretical virtues of simplicity, strength, and fit. These requirements allow the account to rule out 'atypical' results on the grounds of overall theoretical considerations.

The second common objectivist interpretation takes probabilities to be *propensities* that are inherent in objects. Propensities are dispositions or tendencies or powers to yield an outcome, and the strength of the propensity is described (or quantified) by the probability. On this interpretation, there is a tendency inherent in the die to produce the number three, and this tendency has strength 1/6. Different versions of the interpretation differ in what account of powers they give, and a large array of options is available. A problem that all propensity accounts have is that they do not seem to be compatible with determinism: either processes are fundamentally driven by 'chancy' powers, or they are

---

What follows is only the briefest of sketches. Extended discussion can be found in Galavotti (2005) and Gillies (2000); for a discussion of Best Systems accounts, see Hoefer (2019).

deterministic, but not both.[20] This is obviously a problem in the context of SM, where, as we have seen, the underlying dynamics is deterministic.

Subjectivists, also known as Bayesians, think that both frequentism and the propensity interpretations got started on the wrong foot because probabilities are not descriptions of fact but rather descriptions of the state of mind of an agent. The probabilities we attach to outcomes codify the degree of belief, or credence, that an agent has about a certain outcome. To a subjectivist, the statement that the probability for the number three is 1/6 means that an agent's degree of belief that the number three will appear is 1/6. Subjectivists fall into two groups. *Personalist Bayesians* hold that probabilities are nothing over and above the credences of suitable agents, and it is then perfectly conceivable that two agents disagree on their probability assignments. This is what *objective Bayesians* reject.[21] They insist that while probabilities are degrees of belief, probabilities cannot vary across rational agents and are uniquely determined by the available evidence and objective methods of determining probabilities. Among those methods, the maximum entropy principle plays an important role. The principle says that in a situation of lack of knowledge, or *ignorance*, a rational agent should set their credences so that the entropy of their probability distribution is maximal. We will encounter this principle again in Section 4.7.

2.7 Points of Contact

Looking back at the subsections in this section, the reader may be left under the impression that mechanics and probability theory are wholly different and unrelated subject matters. There is a grain of truth in this: the two theories have developed autonomously, and they can be (and are) practiced independently from each other. However, the two theories make contact at two points. The first point of contact is the fact that the state space X of a dynamical system can be regarded as the event space Ω of a probability space, and subsets of X can form its sigma algebra Σ. Indeed, this the standard move in SM, where the events of interest are events in the state space such as 'the system is in state x' or 'the state of the system lies in blob A'. The second point of contact is the measure μ. In Section 2.5 we noted that the measure can be normalised without loss of generality. But a normalised measure has the mathematical structure of a probability. It is therefore no coincidence that in SM μ is often used to provide probabilities of events. Hence, despite

---

[20] For a discussion of chance and determinism, see Frigg (2016).

[21] The label 'objective Bayesian' is somewhat unfortunate because this is obviously not an objective interpretation in the sense in which frequencies and propensities are.

being different theories, the associations of X with Ω and of μ with p provide a strong bridge between the two theories. Indeed, much of SM can be seen as the attempt to articulate the exact nature of this bridge and to show how it works. The main challenge in this endeavour is the handling of the time evolution function ϕ_t. Not only does this function have no 'cousin' in probability theory; it in fact seems to conflict with probability theory in that it introduces structures like trajectories and invariant surfaces on X that are foreign to probability theory, where there is no dynamics on Ω. As a result, a major challenge for SM is to 'harmonise' the way probabilities are introduced with the dynamics of the system. As we will see, different approaches do this in different ways.

3 Boltzmannian Statistical Mechanics

In current debates about SM, 'BSM' denotes a family of positions that take as their starting point the approach that was first introduced by Boltzmann in his (1877) and then presented in a streamlined form by Ehrenfest and Ehrenfest-Afanassjewa in their (1912/1959). In this section we discuss different contemporary articulations of BSM along with the challenges they face.

The section is structured as follows. We begin by introducing the basic structure of BSM that all positions that identify as 'Boltzmannian' share (Section 3.1). We then discuss Boltzmann's combinatorial argument, which is the canonical method to construct macro-states and to identify equilibrium (Section 3.2). This method is often combined with an explanation of the approach to equilibrium based on ergodicity (Section 3.3). Any explanation of the approach to equilibrium faces two immediate objections: Loschmidt's objection based on time-reversal invariance and Zermelo's objection based on Poincaré recurrence (Section 3.4). The package of the combinatorial argument and ergodicity faces a number of difficulties, which are resolved in the Residence Time account (Section 3.5). An alternative account aims to explain the approach to equilibrium in terms of typicality (Section 3.6). Probabilities have played no role in the development of BSM up to this point, and we now review different ways of introducing probabilities into the theory (Section 3.7). The Mentaculus is a distinctive way of resolving some of the issues that arise in BSM, which has at its core the use of conditional probabilities combined with what has become known as the Past Hypothesis (Section 3.8). Despite its appeal, the framework of BSM faces a number of problems and limitations (Section 3.9).

3.1 The Bare Bones of BSM

All positions that gather under the umbrella of BSM share a theoretical core, and different versions of BSM vary in how they develop this core and in what they add to it. In this section we introduce this core.[22]

Boltzmannian SM distinguishes between micro-states and macro-states. The *micro-state* of a system specifies the exact mechanical state of every micro-constituent of the system. As we have seen in Section 2.1, the system's state space X consists of all states that the system could assume. So the system's micro-state at time t is simply the state $x \in X$ in which the system is at time t. Intuitively, the *macro-state* M of a system specifies the macro-constitution of the system in terms of variables like volume, local pressure, local temperature, and other properties that are observable, loosely speaking, at a human scale. The configurations shown in Figure 1 are macro-states in this sense. It is not obvious how to characterise macro-states precisely, and we will come back to this problem in Section 3.9. For now, we operate with an intuitive notion of macro-states.

The core posit of BSM is that macro-states supervene on micro-states. Consider two sets of properties, A and B. A *supervenes* on B if and only if two things cannot differ in their A-properties without also differing in their B-properties.[23] A paradigmatic example comes from the philosophy of mind, where A is the set of mental properties and B is the set of brain properties. Supervenience then says that two people cannot have different mental properties without also having different brain properties. Boltzmannian SM posits that the relation between macro-states and micro-states is just like this: two systems cannot be in different macro-states without also being in different micro-states. Or, in other words, it cannot be that the position and momenta of all molecules in two gases are identical while the macro-conditions of the two gases are different. For this reason, every micro-state x has exactly one corresponding macro-state, which we call $M(x)$.

The correspondence between micro-states and macro-states typically is not one-to-one: several micro-states can correspond to the same macro-state, meaning that macro-states are *multiply realisable*. If, for instance, we swap the positions and momenta of two molecules, the macro-state of the gas does not change. It is then natural to group together all micro-states x that correspond to the same macro-state M: $X_M = \{x \in X \text{ such that } M(x) = M\}$. X_M is the

---

[22] For discussion, see, for instance, Albert (2000), Frigg (2008b), and Goldstein (2001).

[23] This basic idea can be developed in different ways, but nothing in our discussion depends on these differences. For a survey, see McLaughlin and Bennett (2021).

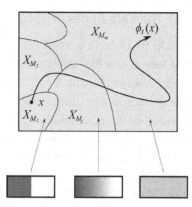

Figure 6 The state space X with the partition of macro-regions.

macro-region of M, which, by definition, contains all and only those micro-states that correspond to macro-state M.

Now consider a complete set of macro-states: a set that contains every macro-state that the system can be in. To keep things simple, assume that there is only a finite number m of such states.[24] Let this complete set be $\{M_1, \ldots, M_m\}$. It is then the case that the set of corresponding macro-regions, $\{X_{M_1}, \ldots, X_{M_m}\}$, forms a partition of X, meaning that the elements of the set do not overlap and jointly cover X. This is illustrated in Figure 6. As in Figure 2, the large square symbolises the state space X, and the curved thin lines symbolise the partition of the state space into different macro-regions. Figure 6 also shows that if the system under study is a gas, then the macro-states correspond to the different states of the gas we encountered in Section 1.1.

This raises two fundamental issues that occupy centre stage in discussions about BSM. The first issue concerns the nature and origin of macro-states. In the previous paragraph we simply postulated that there is a complete set $\{M_1, \ldots, M_m\}$ of macro-states along with the corresponding set $\{X_{M_1}, \ldots, X_{M_m}\}$ of macro-regions. But what is the nature of these macro-states and where do these come from? And there is also a question about the structure of these sets. As we have seen earlier, systems, when prepared in a non-equilibrium state and then left to themselves, approach equilibrium. This means that one of the macro-states in our set must be the equilibrium state. How is this state identified, and what are its characteristics? As we have seen in Section 2.1, the state space X comes equipped with a measure μ that allows us to say how large a part of X is. This measure can now be used to attribute a size to

---

[24] This assumption holds true in the most common way to construct macro-states, which we discuss in the next section. In general, this is an idealisation and systems can have an infinite number of macro-states. Nothing in this section depends on the number of macro-states being finite.

the macro-regions and, as we will see later, it turns out to be the case that equilibrium is the macro-state with the largest macro-region. Hence, the evolution from non-equilibrium to equilibrium can be understood as the evolution from a smaller to larger macro-region. This is indicated in Figure 6, where the largest macro state, X_{M_m}, corresponds to the equilibrium state of the gas, and the smallest to its initial state.

The second issue concerns the approach to equilibrium. In the framework we have outlined so far, an approach to equilibrium takes place if the time evolution of the system is such that a micro-state x in a non-equilibrium macro-region evolves so that $\phi_t(x)$ comes to lie in the equilibrium macro-region at a later point in time, as also illustrated in Figure 6. Ideally, one would want this to happen for all x in any non-equilibrium macro-region, because this would mean that all non-equilibrium states would eventually approach equilibrium. The question now is under what conditions this would be the case, and indeed, whether this is possible at all.

Before turning to these questions, let us introduce the *Boltzmann entropy* S_B, which is a property of macro-states defined through the measures of their macro-regions: $S_B(M_i) = k_B\log[\mu(X_{M_i})]$ for all $i = 1, \ldots, m$, where k_B is the so-called Boltzmann constant. Since a system is in exactly one macro-state at any instant of time, the Boltzmann entropy can equally be regarded as a property of a system itself. Let $M(x(t))$ be the macro-state of the system at time t. The Boltzmann entropy of the system at time t then simply is the Boltzmann entropy of $M(x(t))$. Since the logarithm is a monotonic function, the larger the measure μ of a macro-region, the larger the entropy of the corresponding macro-state. This implies that if the equilibrium macro-state has the largest macro-region, then it also has the highest Boltzmann entropy. The approach to equilibrium can then be described as a transition from low to high Boltzmann entropy.

This framework is the backbone of positions that identify as 'Boltzmannian'. Differences appear in how the elements of this framework are articulated and in what is added to them. Before moving on, we would like to draw attention to an important issue, which has implications for how the theory is developed. As introduced so far, macro-regions are subsets of the state space X. This is how macro-regions are standardly introduced in the literature, and we follow the convention in this section. However, as we have seen in Section 2.2, the motion of an autonomous Hamiltonian system is confined to the hypersurface X_E, which is a $6n - 1$-dimensional subset of the full $6n$-dimensional state space X. Often – for instance in the case discussed in the next section where the equilibrium is given by the Maxwell–Boltzmann distribution – the equilibrium state depends on the energy of the system (and there also might be further conserved quantities that the equilibrium depends on). This means that all macro-states that the system can potentially visit given a certain initial state are defined *relative to the energy of the system* (and sometimes also relative to the invariant surfaces corresponding to other conserved quantities). In such cases, when trying to find the equilibrium state, one has to consider macro-regions that lie in X_E rather than in X and work with a measure μ_E on X_E rather than with the measure μ on X (or, again, if there are further invariant surfaces, one has to find the equilibrium macro-state by considering macro-states relative to constant values of all invariant surfaces).[25]

3.2 Defining Equilibrium: The Combinatorial Argument

In his (1877), Boltzmann presented an ingenious way to address the first issue mentioned in the previous section, to construct macro-states and to identify equilibrium. Boltzmann's argument focuses on the state space of *one* particle of the system, which in the case of a gas has six dimensions. Since the gas is confined to a box, the particles cannot move beyond the box and their energy is bounded (no particle can have more than the total energy of the gas). This means that the particle can access only a finite region of its state space. This is the *accessible region*. This is schematically represented in Figure 7, where the large rectangle symbolises the accessible region (and beware of the schematic character of this figure: we can only draw one p and one q axis, but the space has three p and three q axes). The micro-state of a system is a specification of the position and momenta of all particles. As we

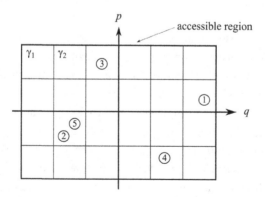

Figure 7 Coarse-graining on the one-particle space.

---

[25] For a more detailed discussion of the role of macro-regions and measures on subsets of X when determining the equilibrium state, see Werndl and Frigg (2015a). In this context, note that the measure μ on X can be restricted to X_E in a natural way; for technical details, see Frigg (2008b, 180).

have seen, in the 'full' $6n$-dimensional state space X this state is given by one point. But this is not the only way to specify the state. We can equally specify the state with n points in the 6-dimensional one-particle space. This is also illustrated in Figure 7, where the numbered circles indicate the state of the particles: the centre of the circle with number 1 denotes the state of particle number 1, and so on.

The crucial move now is to introduce a grid on the space – an operation known as *coarse-graining*. This grid defines *coarse-grained micro-states*: two particles have the same coarse-grained micro-state if they are in the same grid cell. We label the grid cells γ_1, γ_2, ... The cells are such that they all have the same size. A specification of the coarse-grained micro-state of every particle in the system is called an *arrangement*. That is, an arrangement is a list with n entries of the following form: particle number 1 is cell γ_{56}, particle number 2 is in cell γ_{21}, and so on. Again, this is illustrated in Figure 7. At this point there is a crucial realisation: if we are only interested in the macro properties of the gas, then an arrangement contains too much information. This is because it is irrelevant for the system's macro features which particle is in which state. Whether particle number 1 is in cell γ_{56} and particle number 2 is in cell γ_{21}, or vice versa, has no effect on quantities like the local pressure of the gas. This means that the macro-state of the gas must be unaffected by a permutation of the particles. This means that the macro-state of the gas only depends on the *distribution* of particles, a specification of how many particles there are in each grid cell.

The core idea of Boltzmann's approach is to determine how many arrangements are compatible with a given distribution, and to define the equilibrium state as the one for which this number is maximal. To this end, let us introduce n_i, the number of particles in cell γ_i, for all cells. Hence, a distribution D is a vector $(n_1, \ldots, n_k)$, where k is the number of coarse-grained micro-states. Some elementary combinatorics then shows that the number of arrangements that are compatible with a given distribution D is

$$G(D) = \frac{n!}{n_1! \times \ldots \times n_k!},$$

where the exclamation mark denotes the factorial (i.e. $n! = 1 \times 2 \times \ldots \times n$). Making the strong (and, as we will see, unrealistic) assumption that the particles in the gas are non-interacting and that the energy of the gas is preserved, Boltzmann showed that the distribution that has the largest number of compatible arrangements is the one for which the n_i satisfy the so-called discrete Maxwell–Boltzmann distribution:

$$n_i = \alpha \exp(-\beta E_i),$$

where E_i is the energy of particle in cell γ_i, and α and β are constants that depend on the number of particles and the temperature of the system (Tolman 1938/1979, ch. 4). This is the equilibrium distribution of the gas. From a mathematical point of view, deriving this distribution is a problem in combinatorics, which is why the approach is now known as the *combinatorial argument* (Uffink 2007, 974).

The view that the Maxwell–Boltzmann distribution is the equilibrium distribution of the gas receives independent support from an argument due to Maxwell. Indeed, Maxwell had already derived this distribution in his (1860/1965), and, crucially, his derivation is entirely independent from considerations of how many arrangements are compatible with a distribution, and indeed from a choice of coarse-graining on the one-particle space. Maxwell's derivation was based solely on the posit that gas particles move in the same way in all spatial directions and that therefore the distribution function must factorise into functions of the orthogonal components of their velocities. Hence, the equilibrium distribution that the combinatorial argument provides is known to be the equilibrium distribution for reasons that are independent of the combinatorial argument.

These considerations concern the state space of *one* particle. This is different from our considerations so far, which have all been in terms of the $6n$-dimensional state space X of the entire system. So the question is: what does the combinatorial argument tell us about macro-regions in X as introduced in the previous section? The good news is that the results translate. It is obvious that every point in X corresponds to a distribution in the one-particle space (because both specify the position and momenta of all particles). One can then say that all points in X that correspond to the same distribution constitute a macro-region. This is plausible because, as we have seen, the macro properties of the gas only depend on the distribution D. We now need a connection between the number of arrangements compatible with a given distribution and the measure of macro-regions. This connection is provided by the following result:

$$\mu(X_D) = G(D)\Delta^n,$$

where X_D is the macro-region associated with distribution D and Δ is the size of a cell of the coarse-graining (as shown in Figure 7). Hence, the size of a macro-region is proportional to the number of arrangements compatible with the distribution associated with the macro-region. This leads directly to the desired result: since $G(D)$ is maximal for the Maxwell–Boltzmann distribution, the largest macro-region is the one that consists of points that correspond to that distribution.[26] This justifies the posit that we should regard the largest macro-region as the equilibrium macro-region.[27]

Its ingenuity notwithstanding, the combinatorial argument faces a number of serious issues, both technical and conceptual. The first is a consequence of the assumption, highlighted earlier, that the particles in the gas are non-interacting, which also implies that particles never collide. So, strictly speaking, the argument only applies to a so-called *ideal gas*, a gas that, by definition, consists only of non-interacting particles. There are no ideal gases in nature, and so the macro-state structure that results from the argument is not a true description of any real-world system. One may say that this does not detract from its usefulness because the ideal gas is a reasonable approximation of a *dilute gas*, a gas that has a low density and in which collisions are relatively infrequent. Even if one grants this point, this is a serious limitation. While dilute gases are paradigmatic examples of SM systems, the scope of the theory is much larger than that. Important applications of SM are to interacting systems like liquids and solids, and such systems are not like ideal gases, not even approximately. The behaviour both of solids and liquids (and even of dense gases) essentially depends on the interaction between their micro-constituents, and a theory that is forced to idealise these interactions away is bound to miss out on what is essential to how real systems behave.

But what about Maxwell's derivation? Does it not show that the Maxwell–Boltzmann distribution is the equilibrium distribution of a gas? Yes, it does. But it does so under the same idealisation of non-interaction as Boltzmann's argument. That Maxwell could derive the distribution from assumptions that are different than Boltzmann's is remarkable in many ways, but it does nothing to broaden the scope of the theory, which remains confined to ideal (and near-ideal) gases.

The next issue concerns coarse-graining. As we have seen, the argument relies on putting a specific grid on the one-particle space. And the specific grid is essential, because the distributions and the arrangements that drive the argument are defined in terms of the grid cells that we have seen earlier. Furthermore, one can show that the argument does not give the correct results for another kind of grid, namely when one instead partitions the energy levels of

---

[26] The notion of being 'large' is ambiguous between being the largest part of X and being larger than any other macro-region. The former is known as 'dominance' and the latter as 'prevalence'. Both are relevant in BSM, but in different ways. For further discussion, see Werndl and Frigg (2015a).

[27] Further to the observation in the last paragraph of Section 3.1, if one defines macro-regions relative to X_E, then the macro-regions are the intersection of X_E with the areas identified in the combinatorial argument. For details, see Frigg (2008b, 112–13).

the particles (Uffink 2007, 977). This raises two questions. Prima facie, it seems to be rather arbitrary to cut up the one-particle state space into different cells and engage in combinatorial thinking with these cells. So, the first question is: what justifies the choice of a grid to begin with? As noted, not all coarse-grainings yield the correct result. So the second question is: what justifies the choice of the particular grid with a partition along the position and momentum axes with cells of equal size?

As regards the first question, one could try to justify the use of coarse-graining by appeal to limited knowledge. Since measurement instruments invariably have a finite resolution, we can never observe the exact value of a physical quantity. This means that we can never know the position and the momentum of particles precisely; all we can assert is that the result lies within a certain range. If we choose the grid so that the cell size reflects the precision with which we can know the position and momentum of a particle, then the coarse-graining can be interpreted as a natural reflection on our epistemic limitations.[28] We will discuss justifications based on epistemic considerations in more detail in Section 4.5, but we want to flag here that such justifications are ultimately unconvincing. The equilibrium properties of a system are physical properties in the world and as such do not depend on what we know (or even can possibly know) about the system. A system would have an equilibrium state, and approach that state, even if there were no sentient observers at all, and therefore its construction cannot be dependent on epistemic considerations.

This suggests that one might try to regard coarse-graining as an expedient but ultimately dispensable mathematical ploy. For this strategy to work, one would have to be able to get rid of the coarse-graining by making the grid smaller and smaller until it vanishes. From a mathematical point of view this means that one would have to be able to take the limit $\Delta \rightarrow 0$, and the Maxwell–Boltzmann distribution would have to be stable under the limiting procedure. This is not the case. In fact, the combinatorial argument tacitly assumes that the number n of particles in the gas is much larger than the number k of coarse-grained micro-states, which ensures that all n_j are large. Once we get to the point where there are more coarse-grained micro-states than particles (which unavoidably happens in the limit $\Delta \rightarrow 0$), each state will be occupied either by only one particle or by none. At this point distributions become trivial in that all n_j are either zero or one (and the number of arrangements compatible with a given distribution is always n). This is not the Maxwell–Boltzmann distribution, and so one does not

---

[28] One might even argue that the minimal size of a cell is given by the quantum mechanical uncertainty relations.

recover the correct equilibrium distribution for the limit $\Delta \rightarrow 0$. This shows that having a finite grid with a k that is much smaller than n is a necessary condition for the argument to get off the ground, and so the grid is not a dispensable expedient.

Hence, there is no convincing justification of the appeal to coarse-graining. And things do not look better as regards the second question, the quest of a justification of the particular coarse-graining in the combinatorial argument. One might say that the justification lies in the fact that it provides the correct result. But this would seem to be a bit too anaemic. Coarse-grainings are conceptually foreign to Hamiltonian mechanics, which works with a continuous state space. If a particular grid is put on that state space to provide the crucial result, then one would want to have an explanation of why this and not another grid provides the correct result. As far as we know, no such explanation is currently available.

The combinatorial argument also faces a more conceptual quandary. In our presentation of BSM in Section 3.1 we started with macro-states $\{M_1, ..., M_m\}$ and then used the postulate that macro-states supervene on micro-states to determine the macro-regions $\{X_{M_1}, ..., X_{M_m}\}$. The combinatorial argument reverses this order by constructing macro-regions directly without saying anything about what the macro-states and the macro-properties themselves look like. This disconnect is particularly striking in the case of equilibrium. A typical thermodynamics textbook definition of equilibrium is that a 'thermodynamic system is in equilibrium when none of its thermodynamic properties are changing with time' (Reiss 1965, 3), and this is in line with our introductory example in Section 1.1, where we said that the gas has reached equilibrium when the gas is evenly spread out and no further change takes place. This has very little, if anything, in common with the kind of considerations underlying the combinatorial argument, where the equilibrium macro-state is the one whose distribution is compatible with the largest number of arrangements. What is the conceptual connection between these two ways of framing equilibrium?

Finally, the combinatorial definition of equilibrium is completely disconnected from the dynamics of the system. This is out of sync both with our introductory example and with thermodynamics, where, as we have just seen, equilibrium is seen as the final state of the autonomous time evolution of the system. Divorcing a definition of equilibrium from the dynamics of the system has the odd consequence that the combinatorial argument would still provide an equilibrium state even if the time evolution of the system was the identity function (and hence nothing would ever change, and no approach to equilibrium would take place).

3.3 The Approach to Equilibrium: The Ergodic Account

As we have just seen, the notion of equilibrium provided by the combinatorial argument remains silent about the temporal evolution of a system, and so we need an additional dynamical assumption to ensure that the system behaves thermodynamically. In their review of SM, Ehrenfest and Ehrenfest-Afanassjewa ('the Ehrenfests' henceforth) highlight this problem: they note that there is gap between the fact that the macro-region corresponding to the Maxwell–Boltzmann distribution is the largest macro-region and the claim that the system approaches equilibrium and spends most of its time in equilibrium (1912/1959, 30–31). They then note that this gap can be bridged by assuming that the system is ergodic.[29] As we have seen in Section 2.5, if a system is ergodic, then, for almost all initial conditions, the fraction of time the system spends in a subset A of X is equal to the proportion of A in X. We are of course free to take A to be the equilibrium macro-region. According to the combinatorial argument, the equilibrium macro-region is the largest macro-region in X, and so it follows immediately that if the system is ergodic, it will spend most of its time in equilibrium for almost all initial conditions. This is the ergodic account of the approach to equilibrium.

The ergodic account faces a number of problems. Some of them are rooted in the general structure of Hamiltonian systems and we will discuss these in the next section. At this point we want to mention two problems that stem directly from the notion of ergodicity. The first problem is that being ergodic is a stringent condition that many systems fail to meet. This is worrying because among those systems are many to which SM is successfully applied. For instance, in a solid the molecules oscillate around fixed positions in a lattice, and as a result the phase point of the system can only access a small part of the energy hypersurface (Uffink 2007, 1017). The Kac ring model and a system of anharmonic oscillators behave thermodynamically but fail to be ergodic (Bricmont 2001). And even the ideal gas – one of the paradigm systems of SM – is not ergodic (Uffink 1996b, 381). But if core systems of SM are not ergodic, then ergodicity cannot provide an explanation for the approach to equilibrium, at least not one that is applicable across the board (Earman and Rédei 1996; van Lith 2001).[30]

---

[29] For a discussion of Boltzmann's original hypothesis and its problems see Sklar (1993, 159–62).
[30] Attempts have been made to improve the situation through the notion of epsilon-ergodicity. A system is epsilon-ergodic if it is ergodic only on subset $Y \subset X$ where $\mu(Y) \geq 1 - \varepsilon$, for a small positive real number ε (Vranas 1998). While this approach deals successfully with some systems (Frigg and Werndl 2011), it is still not universally applicable and hence remains silent about large classes of SM systems.

The second worry is of a more technical nature and is known as the *measure zero problem*. As we have seen, ergodicity says that 'almost all initial conditions' are such that the fraction of time spent in A is equal to the fraction A occupies in X. This means that that there is a set of initial conditions for which this need not be the case, and that this set has measure zero (with respect to μ). Intuitively this would seem to suggest that these conditions are negligible. However, as Sklar (1993, 182–88) points out, sets of measure zero can be rather large (remember that the set of rational numbers has measure zero in the real numbers), and the problem is to justify why a set of measure zero really is negligible.

3.4 Two Objections: Loschmidt and Zermelo

Some readers may have noticed that a surreptitious shift in the aims of SM has occurred at the beginning of the previous section. When introducing the notion of equilibrium in Section 1.1, we said that the gas has reached equilibrium when the spreading has come to an end and no further change takes place. In terms of the macro-regions introduced in Section 3.1 this means that the system would have to evolve into the equilibrium macro-region and then stay there forever. In the previous section a different quality was presented as the desired result of the investigation, namely that the system will spend most of its time in equilibrium for almost all initial conditions. This is obviously a more modest aim because spending most of the time in the equilibrium region is compatible with the system moving *out of equilibrium* every now and then, which is impossible if there must be no further change once the system has reached equilibrium. This is not a slip. The shift is deliberate. In the first instance it is a concession to ergodicity because the more modest result is what ergodicity provides. But the reasons for adopting the shift cut deeper: the structure of Hamiltonian mechanics (Section 2.2) prevents *any* account of SM (irrespective of whether it appeals to ergodicity) from ever providing more. Spending most of the time in the equilibrium region is the best that one can hope for in a Hamiltonian system. This is for two reasons.

The first reason is time-reversal invariance. Hamiltonian mechanics is time-reversal invariant, and, as we have seen in Section 2.3, this means that if a process from an initial state $(q_i, \; p_i)$ to a final state $(q_f, \; p_f)$ during timespan Δt is allowed, then a process starting in state $(q_f, -p_f)$ and ending in state $(q_i, -p_i)$ during timespan Δt is allowed too. Now look at Figure 6. The initial condition x in the bottom left is $(q_i, \; p_i)$ and the tip of the arrow is $(q_f, \; p_f)$. The trajectory indicates that the transition from $(q_i, \; p_i)$ to $(q_f, \; p_f)$ is allowed. This means that the transition from $(q_f, -p_f)$ to $(q_i, -p_i)$ is allowed too. Let us now assume that macro-regions are invariant under time reversal: if a state (q, p) is in macro-region X_M, the time-reversed state $(q, -p)$ also is in macro-region X_M.[31] It then follows that if the transition (shown in Figure 6) from a small non-equilibrium macro-region to the equilibrium macro-region is allowed by the theory, then the reverse evolution, from the equilibrium macro-region into the small non-equilibrium macro-region, is allowed too. In other words: systems are allowed to evolve out of equilibrium. This observation is known as *Loschmidt's reversibility objection* because it was first put forward by Loschmidt (1876).[32]

The second reason is Poincaré recurrence. As we have seen in Section 2.4, systems with a state space of finite measure and a dynamics that is measure preserving show Poincaré recurrence, and Poincaré recurrence implies that for almost all initial conditions, the system will return arbitrarily close to the initial condition infinitely many times. SM systems satisfy the conditions of the theorem. This implies that for almost all initial conditions in a non-equilibrium macro-region like the one in Figure 6, the system will eventually return arbitrarily close to it. This implies that the system will return to the initial macro-state. This is known as *Zermelo's recurrence objection* because it was first put forward by Zermelo (1896).[33]

In Section 1.1 we said that a key characteristic of the approach to equilibrium was that it seems to be *irreversible*: systems move from non-equilibrium to equilibrium, but not vice versa. Both objections cut against irreversibility. Indeed, they show that the approach to equilibrium cannot possibly be irreversible (at least as long as the system is Hamiltonian).[34] So, the structure of Hamiltonian mechanics forces us to reject the requirement of irreversibility, which turns out to be too stringent a requirement. But if not irreversibility, what requirement should systems in SM satisfy? The next best to irreversibility would seem to be the requirement that systems, when prepared in a non-equilibrium macro-state, approach equilibrium and then spend most of their time in equilibrium (although fluctuations away from equilibrium are permitted so long as they are brief). Hence, what SM should explain is not strict irreversibility, but the fact that systems spend most of the time in equilibrium. The ergodic approach does this by construction.

---

[31] We note that it is not a general feature of macro-regions that they are time-reversal invariant. But it seems to be an assumption in the literature on the subject that the macro-regions we are interested in happen to be time-reversal invariant.

[32] For a historical discussion of this objection, see Darrigol (2021).

[33] For a historical discussion, see Uffink (2007).

[34] Considerations of this kind led Krylov to argue that SM cannot be founded on Hamiltonian mechanics. For a discussion, see Rédei (1992).

3.5 The Residence Time Account

Let us take stock. We constructed macro-regions with the combinatorial argument and appealed to ergodicity to explain why systems are in equilibrium most of the time in the long run. We were able to dispel concerns about the absence of irreversibility, and we established the requirement that systems approach equilibrium and then spend most of their time in equilibrium as the reasonable goal of SM. These successes notwithstanding, the account that has emerged so far suffers from serious difficulties. The definition of the equilibrium state through the combinatorial argument relies on a physically unmotivated partition; its scope is limited to non-interacting systems; and its notion of equilibrium is disconnected from the thermodynamic notion of equilibrium and independent of the dynamics (and hence also provides an equilibrium state in situations in which it should not, for instance, when the dynamics is the identity function). The approach to equilibrium relies on the condition that systems be ergodic, which many important SM systems fail to meet.

This should give us pause. One cannot rule out that the proofs of the arguments in Sections 3.2 and 3.3 can be altered and generalised in ways that avoid these problems. But prospects look dim: not only are no such generalisations known; it is indeed unclear where one would look for them. For this reason, it would certainly be better not to have these problems to begin with. Avoiding these problems while – somehow – retaining the important tenets of the approach that we have discussed so far is the aim of the *residence time account*, or RT account, for short (Werndl and Frigg 2015a, 2015b).

The central result we get from the combinatorial argument combined with ergodicity is that, in the long run, the system spends most of its time in equilibrium. The core idea of the RT account is to reverse the order of explanation and take this as a point of departure rather than deriving it from the combinatorial argument plus ergodicity. That is, the RT account takes the observation that a system spends most of its time in equilibrium to be the *definition* of equilibrium and aims to retrieve other results (for instance, that the equilibrium macro-region is the largest macro-region and that ergodic systems behave thermodynamically) as consequences of the approach.

To develop this idea, let us introduce some notation. Consider a macro-state M and an initial condition x at time t_0 (which are as we have seen in Figure 6). Then let $f_{M,x}$ be the fraction of time that a system with initial condition x spends in the macro-region X_M in the long run (i.e. for $t \to \infty$), where the fraction of time is understood in the same way as in the context of the ergodic account (see Sections 2.5 and 3.3). In Section 2.5 we encountered the characteristic function of a set A in X: the function assumes value 1 for x that are in A and 0 for x outside

A. We can now choose *A* to be the macro-region X_M, and so the function assumes value 1 for *x* that are in X_M and 0 for *x* outside X_M. Let us call this function $\chi_M(x)$. Now recall Equation (2), which gives us the time average of a function. Plugging $\chi_M(x)$ into that equation immediately yields

$$f_{M,x} = \lim_{\tau \to \infty} \int_{t_0}^{t_0+\tau} \chi_M(\phi_t(x))dt.$$

All $f_{M,x}$ lie in the interval [0, 1]. The time a system spends in *M* is the *residence time* of the system in *M*, and $f_{M,x}$ is the long-run fraction of the residence time. This gives the approach its name.

Next, let us introduce a parameter α that quantifies what fraction of time the system spends in equilibrium in the long run. As we have seen, a system is expected to spend most of its time in equilibrium. So we would expect α to be close to one. However, there is a vexed question about how close is close enough. At this point we take a minimal stance on this and only say that it must be more than 0.5. The RT account covers all values α ∈ (0.5, 1], and hence one can always choose a specific value for α that meets further requirements.

A first attempt to implement the idea announced earlier would be to say that if the system has a micro-state *M* for which $f_{M,x} \geq α$ for some α ∈ (0.5, 1] and for all *x*, then this macro-state is the equilibrium state of the system. This is on the right track, but a further refinement is needed. As we have seen in the discussion of ergodicity, not all initial conditions lie on trajectories that behave ergodically. In fact, there can be a set of measure zero consisting of initial conditions that behave differently. It is reasonable to make similar allowances here and not require that $f_{M,x} \geq α$ for all *x*. Indeed, we want to be even more liberal than the ergodic approach and not require that the set of 'bad' conditions has to be of measure zero; instead, we allow for sets that have a finite albeit small measure ε (i.e. $0 \leq ε \ll 1$). This amounts to saying that we require the system to behave 'correctly' on a subset *Y* of *X* which is such that $\mu(Y) \geq 1 - ε$.

We are now in the position to give a definition of equilibrium: an equilibrium exists when there is a *Y* (with $\mu(Y) \geq 1 - ε$) such that the system has a macro-state *M* which satisfies the condition $f_{M,x} \geq α$ for all *x* ∈ *Y*. To make explicit that equilibrium thus defined depends on the values of the two parameters α and ε one can also call this an α-ε-equilibrium, but we will mostly just call it 'equilibrium' for brevity.[35]

---

[35] As noted in footnote 26, 'large' is ambiguous. This definition is based on macro-regions being large in the sense of dominance. For a definition of equilibrium based on large in the sense of prevalence, see Werndl and Frigg (2015a).

It is important to note that this definition is phrased in terms of the *time* a system spends in the state we call equilibrium. This is at odds with the way in which we introduced equilibrium in Section 3.1, where we said that equilibrium was the state with the largest macro-region, which is a definition in terms of *size*. Have we left the Boltzmannian framework? No. In fact, one can prove that if M is an α-ε-equilibrium macro-state, then $\mu(X_M) \geq \alpha(1 - \varepsilon)$. Since α is usually close to one and ε close to zero, $\alpha(1 - \varepsilon)$ is close to one too (Werndl and Frigg 2015b). Recall that we assumed the state space to be normalised (i.e. $\mu(X) = 1$), and so this means that the equilibrium macro-region is large, as BSM would have it. Hence, we have recovered, *as a theorem*, the posit of BSM that the equilibrium state is large in X.

But, some will now ask, what is the advantage of this account over the combinatorial argument, which also provides the result that the equilibrium macro-region is large? The answer is that the RT account has managed to shed the most important limitations and problems of the combinatorial argument. First, the RT account is *completely general* in that no assumptions about particles and their interactions are needed. Second, it does not require a partition of the one-particle state space and so there is no question about how to justify the choice of a grid. Third, as we have seen, it is a problem for the combinatorial argument that its notion of equilibrium is completely discon-nected from the dynamics (it provides us with an equilibrium state even if nothing moves). The RT account solves this problem by building the approach to equilibrium into the definition of an equilibrium: an equilibrium exists only if the dynamics and the macro-state structure are such that there is a macro-state in which the system spends most of its time for nearly all initial conditions.[36] Finally, the RT account does not require dynamical conditions like ergodicity, and hence avoids the difficulty that many systems may not be ergodic.

This makes the existence (and nature) of an equilibrium state dependent not only on the size of the macro-region in the state space, but also on the behaviour of the system over time. That is, whether a macro-state with a large macro-region is also an equilibrium state not only depends on the intrinsic features of the macro-state, but also on the dynamics of the system. This has the conse-quence that the macro-state characterised by the Maxwell–Boltzmann distribu-tion may not be the equilibrium state in certain systems. In our view, this is the correct verdict. Consider again the example of a system whose dynamics is given by the identity function. In such a system no state that is not initially in the macro-region characterised by the Maxwell–Boltzmann distribution will ever move into it. In such a case it seems bizarre to call this region the equilibrium

---

[36] So the account incorporates the minus-first law of TD, which we mentioned in Section 1.1.

region. In general, an equilibrium state that the system never assumes, or that it assumes only for a short time, is an oxymoron.

Does this mean that the combinatorial argument and the ergodic approach have become obsolete? No, but in the RT account they assume a different role. The RT account merely states the general conditions for a system to have an equilibrium. It does not identify specific systems that meet these conditions, nor does it characterise their details. One can see the combinatorial argument and the ergodic approach as doing that. If the dynamics is ergodic, the macro-region defined by Maxwell–Boltzmann distribution, X_{MB}, is an equilibrium state in the sense of the RT account because the state meets the condition for $\varepsilon = 0$ and $\alpha = \mu(X_{MB})$. Hence such a system is a concrete instance of a system with an equilibrium in the sense of the RT account. But, and this is the crucial point, it is only an instance. There will be other systems that meet the conditions, and these systems can be very different from the systems defined through the combinatorial argument plus ergodicity. So what was initially presented as the whole of SM turns out to be just a special case. This solves the problem of the unrealistic nature of the idealising assumptions in the combinatorial argument. If we do not expect all systems in SM to fall under the scope of the combinatorial argument, there is no problem with idealising assumptions that other systems do not meet.

As we have just seen, the RT account provides general conditions on an equilibrium state. This raises the question of the circumstances under which an equilibrium exists. The account answers this question by providing a general existence theorem (Werndl and Frigg 2015a, 2023). As we have seen in Section 2.5, the ergodic decomposition theorem says that *every* system of the kind we are considering in SM – irrespective of whether it is ergodic on X – has a unique ergodic decomposition, meaning that its state space can be divided into different parts so that the dynamics is ergodic on each part. Intuitively, the existence theorem then says that there is an equilibrium just in case the ergodic decomposition of the system is such that the equilibrium macro-state is largest in size *on each part of the ergodic decomposition.*[37] The last clause is crucial. A macro-region can be large but not correspond to an equilibrium state because it is located entirely in one part of the decomposition, and if the initial condition of the system lies in other parts of the decomposition, the system will never move into that region, no matter how large it is. One can then show that standard examples of SM systems such as the Kac ring and the Baker's gas that are not covered by the combinatorial argument do indeed meet this condition and hence

---

[37] To be precise, this has to hold with the exception of those parts of the ergodic decomposition that are contained in the set $X \backslash Y$ of exceptional initial conditions which are not required to approach equilibrium.

have equilibria in the preceding sense (Werndl and Frigg 2015b). This theorem re-orientates the discussion about equilibrium, which should focus on finding combinations of macro-states and dynamical conditions that satisfy the conditions of the existence theorem. Finding and describing at least some of them is a new research programme in the foundation of statistical mechanics that will shed light on why and how systems behave thermodynamically.

3.6 Typicality

An alternative account aims to explain the approach to equilibrium in terms of *typicality*. Intuitively, something is typical if it happens in the vast majority of cases: typical lottery tickets are blanks, typical members of an orchestra have undergone extensive musical training, and in a typical series of a thousand coin tosses the ratio of the number of heads and the number of tails is approximately one. As we have seen in previous sections, the macro-region of the equilibrium macro-state is much larger than the macro-region of non-equilibrium states. Proponents of the typicality account note that numerical considerations show that the measure of the equilibrium macro-region is 10^n times larger than the measure of a non-equilibrium state, and if we bear in mind that the number of molecules of a standard gas is of the order of Avogadro's number (i.e. $n \approx 6 \times 10^{23}$), we realise the discrepancy is huge. The equilibrium macro-region therefore takes up almost the entire state space.[38] This means that equilibrium micro-states are typical in X because most states in X are equilibrium micro-states.

The fact that the equilibrium macro-region is large plays an important role in all accounts we have discussed so far, and so there is no disagreement on this point. The typicality account parts ways with other accounts in its assessment of the work that this fact is doing. The accounts previously discussed see the largeness – or typicality – of the equilibrium macro-region as one component of an explanation of the approach to equilibrium, which, however, must be supplemented with a dynamical condition such as ergodicity. The typicality account objects that such an addition is unnecessary because the typicality of the equilibrium macro-region is by itself sufficient to explain why systems

---

[38] This is the standard gloss in the typicality literature; see, for instance, Goldstein (2001, 43). We note, however, that this claim is not universally true. The formalism only shows that the equilibrium macro-region is larger than *any other macro-region*, but this does not imply that it occupies the largest part of the phase space. In fact, Lavis (2008) showed that there are systems in which the non-equilibrium macro-regions *taken together* are larger than the equilibrium macro-region even though the equilibrium region is larger than any individual non-equilibrium macro-region. In the remainder of this section, we set this issue aside and accept the standard gloss.

approach equilibrium. Goldstein offers the following account of the approach to equilibrium:[39]

> [The energy hypersurface] consists almost entirely of phase points in the equilibrium microstate [...], with ridiculously few exceptions whose totality has volume of order $10^{-10^{20}}$ relative to that of [the energy hypersurface]. For a non-equilibrium phase point [x] of energy E, the Hamiltonian dynamics governing the motion [$x(t)$] would have to be ridiculously special to avoid reasonably quickly carrying [$\phi_t(x)$] into [the equilibrium macro-region] and keeping it there for an extremely long time – unless, of course, [x] itself were ridiculously special. (2001, 43–4)

This passage allows for two readings.[40] On the first reading, the suggestion is that a system approaches equilibrium simply because equilibrium micro-states are typical. This interpretation is consonant with Goldstein's insistence that a reliance on dynamical conditions like the basic notions of ergodic theory, in particular ergodicity and mixing, is 'thoroughly misguided' (Goldstein 2001, 45). It also seems to be Zanghì's view when he insists that 'reaching the equilibrium distribution in the course of the temporal evolution of a system is inevitable due to the fact that the overwhelming majority of micro-states in the phase space have this distribution [i.e. the Maxwell–Boltzmann distribution]' (2005, 196; our translation).

As Uffink notes (2007, 979–80), this position is untenable from the point of view of modern dynamical systems theory. As we have seen in Section 2.2, the time evolution of a system depends on two factors: its initial condition x and its Hamiltonian H. The size of parts of the state space are immaterial to the time evolution of the system, and initial conditions do not evolve into a certain region of the state space just because it is large. Indeed, as we have also seen in Section 2.2, if a system has a conserved quantity, then there is an invariant hypersurface in the state space that no trajectory can ever cross. Looking at Figure 6, it might well be that there exists such a hypersurface separating the macro-region in which the initial condition lies and the equilibrium macro-region, which would prevent the system from ever reaching equilibrium. Whether there is such a hypersurface, and more generally whether the system evolves in a way that carries it into equilibrium, depends not only on the nature of the equilibrium state but also on the dynamics (i.e. the Hamiltonian) of the

---

[39] We here follow Goldstein's (2001) discussion. There is now a sizeable literature on the topic of typicality. For a critical discussion, see Frigg (2009, 2011) and Frigg and Werndl (2012). For recent replies and further discussions, see, for instance, Badino (2020), Bricmont (2022), Maudlin (2020), and Wilhelm (2022).

[40] In fact, there is a third version of the typicality account, due to Lebowitz (1993), which focuses on the internal structure of macro-regions. Mutatis mutandis, this approach faces the same challenges as Goldstein's. For a discussion, see Frigg (2009, 2011).

system. Systems do not evolve into equilibrium simply because the equilibrium macro-region is overwhelmingly large.

The second reading takes this point into account. Indeed, in the preceding quote Goldstein says that the Hamiltonian dynamics would have to be 'ridiculously special' to avoid carrying an initial condition x into the equilibrium macro-region. This clearly is a condition on the dynamics of the system, albeit not a very informative one because Goldstein does not tell us what he means by 'ridiculously special'. Could one just shrug one's shoulders and dismiss this as a technicality of little conceptual or philosophical consequence? No. Indeed, understanding the dynamical conditions that lead to an approach to equilibrium has been one of the core concerns of SM since its inception. The way in which this issue has been discussed has changed over the years: in the nineteenth century the focus was on the nature of collisions, and discussions in the twentieth century have focused on ergodic theory. Much can be said about the different approaches that have been tried, but one cannot exorcise this discussion and pretend that dynamics does not matter.

So the typicality account faces a catch-22: in its simple version (the first reading) the account is in contradiction with Hamiltonian mechanics, and in its more nuanced version (the second reading) it has to do what it was designed to avoid, namely engage with dynamical conditions.

3.7 Where Have Probabilities Gone?

At the beginning of Section 2 we said that SM owes its name to the fact that it aims to integrate mechanics and probability theory into a harmonious whole. But so far probabilities have been notable primarily for their absence. In the statement of the basic framework of BSM in Section 3.1 probabilities were not mentioned at all, and they have not played a role in later sections either. So we may wonder: where have probabilities gone? The absence of probabilities so far is not an oversight. BSM is a theory that focuses on mechanical properties and that sees probabilities as emerging from these. In this section we discuss how probabilities arise from the mechanical properties of BSM systems, and how they can be interpreted.

A first way of introducing probabilities was suggested by Boltzmann in connection with the combinatorial argument. Boltzmann was concerned with the probability of a certain distribution $D = (n_1, \ldots, n_k)$ and stated:

> The probability of this distribution is then given by the number of permutations of which the elements of this distribution are capable, that is by the number $[G(D)]$. As the most probable distribution, i.e. as the one

corresponding to thermal equilibrium, we again regard that distribution for which this expression is maximal [...]. (1877, 187)[41]

In other words, Boltzmann posits that the probability of a certain distribution D, $p(D)$, is proportional to $G(D)$. As we have seen in Section 3.2, distributions determine macro-states, and the size of a macro-state is proportional to $G(D)$ (via the relation $\mu(X_D) = G(D)\ \Delta^n$). So it follows immediately that the probability of a macro-state is proportional to its size: $p(D) = \mu(X_D)$.[42] Let us call this the *proportionality postulate*.

The question now is how these probabilities should be interpreted. As we have seen in Section 2.6, there are three main options available: frequencies, propensities, and credences. For a propensity interpretation one would need to work out a specific account showing how propensities are compatible with the deterministic dynamics of SM systems, and, as noted in Section 2.6, there is a question as to whether this is possible. At any rate, we are not aware of a worked-out account interpreting the probabilities given by the proportionality postulate as propensities. Credences are a possible interpretation, but subjectivism is generally regarded as problematic in the context of SM because the processes SM describes seem to be part of nature and hence would have to unfold as they do irrespective of what someone happens to know about them. We further discuss subjectivism in the context of GSM in Section 4.7.

This leaves frequentism. As we have seen in Section 2.5, if a system is ergodic, the amount of time it spends in a certain region of the state space is equal to the (normalised) measure of that region. Frequencies seem to be closely related to time averages. So, under the assumptions that the system is ergodic and that we can assimilate time averages to frequencies, the probability of a distribution $p(D)$ can be interpreted as the average time that the system spends in D in the long run. The crucial question for this interpretation is whether it is legitimate to regard time averages as a version of frequencies. At first blush, infinite time averages seem to be the 'continuum version' of infinite relative frequencies, which are the core of von Mises' frequentism. However, on closer inspection it turns out that time averages are rather different from relative frequencies, and hence there is a question whether, once all the details are spelled out, they really fit the mould of frequentism.[43] The remaining question then is whether finite frequentism, in particular in its *Humean best systems* version, fits the bill. To the best of our knowledge, this is largely an open question.

---

[41] This and subsequent quotes from Boltzmann are our own translations. Square brackets indicate that Bolzmann's notation has been replaced by the notation used in this Element.
[42] Recall that we assume the measure to be normalised.
[43] For a discussion of this point, see von Plato (1988, 262–5; 1989, 434–7).

Let us set interpretations aside and return to the issue of how to define probabilities in BSM. The proportionality principle anchored probabilities in the size of macro-regions. An entirely different approach is to locate probabilities in the initial conditions. In processes like the spreading of a gas, the system starts in a small macro-region like X_{M_1} (shown in the bottom left corner of Figure 6). Every trajectory has a particular initial condition, and the dynamics specifies how initial conditions evolve in time. The dynamics is, however, silent about where the initial conditions themselves come from. This allows us to say that a system assumes a certain initial condition with a certain probability. Let us call this probability distribution ξ. A common assumption is that the probability of a system having a particular initial condition is simply the measure μ restricted to the initial macro-region. Assuming this region is X_{M_1}, this measure is $\xi = \mu/\mu \ (X_{M_1})$. If μ is the uniform measure over X, then this is the uniform measure over X_{M_1}. An alternative proposal is to prepare the system in the same initial macro-state many times and then fit a probability distribution δ through the initial conditions in which the system happens to be. We then have $\xi = \delta$. The distribution δ may or may not be identical to $\mu/\mu \ (X_{M_1})$.[44] Once one has a probability distribution over initial states, the probability of a system behaving thermodynamically is $\xi(T)$, where T is the subset of X_{M_1} consisting of all initial conditions that lie on trajectories that behave thermodynamically.

As in the preceding account, the next question is how to interpret these probabilities. In principle, all options are on the table, and a propensity interpretation enjoys the advantage that no conflict with determinism has to be resolved because the selection of initial conditions is not governed by the system's deterministic laws. Furthermore, distributions of this kind have been discussed widely in the literature on the *Humean best systems* interpretation of probability, and they do lend themselves to an interpretation in these terms.[45]

3.8 Conditional Probabilities and the Mentaculus

Let us now return to Boltzmann's proportionality postulate. After spelling out the postulate, Boltzmann then aims to explain the approach to equilibrium through systems having a tendency to evolve from unlikely macro-states to more likely macro-states and finally to the most likely macro-state: 'In most cases the initial state will be a very unlikely state. From this state the system will

---

[44] For a discussion of producing probability distributions in this way, see Leeds (1989) and Werndl (2013).

[45] For an interpretation of these probabilities and Humean best systems probabilities, see Frigg and Hoefer (2015).

steadily evolve towards more likely states until it has finally reached the most likely state, i.e. the state of thermal equilibrium' (Boltzmann 1877, 165).

Where does this tendency come from? It does not follow from the probabilities in the proportionality postulate themselves. The probabilities introduced in the proportionality postulate are *unconditional* probabilities, and as such they do not imply anything about the succession of macro-states, let alone that macro-states of low probability are followed by macro-states of higher probability. To illustrate this problem, consider a loaded die which is such that getting number 6 has probability 0.25 and all other numbers have probability 0.15. This reasoning would suggest that after throwing the number four, one would expect to get the number six because it is the more likely number. But this is not the case. In fact, we should expect not to get the number six because getting six is less likely than getting another number. But, a critic might reply, this example is misleading because it does not take into account that the equilibrium state is overwhelmingly more likely than other states. So the die would have to be loaded so that the probability for the number six is 0.99 and the probabilities for the other numbers is 0.002. This does not help. It is now true that we are overwhelmingly likely to get the number six at the next throw, but this has nothing to do with the result of the previous throw. There is no *progression* from less likely to more likely.

What we need to do to make sense of Boltzmann's claims are conditional probabilities. Specifically, we need *temporal* conditional probabilities, also known as *transition probabilities*. Let us begin by introducing these at a general level. Consider two blobs A and B in the state space X as shown in Figure 8 and ask the question: assuming that the state of the system is in A at time t, what is the probability of it being in B at later time $t + \tau$ for some finite time τ? To answer this question, let us introduce the set $\phi_{-\tau}(B)$. Intuitively, this is the set B moved backward in time for the period τ; formally it is the set of all states in X that evolve into B during τ (i.e. $\phi_{-\tau}(B) = \{x \in X : \phi_\tau(x) \in B\}$).

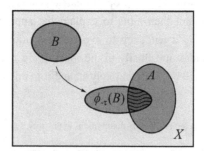

Figure 8 Conditional probabilities in the state space.

Given that the time evolution ϕ_t of the system is deterministic, all states that were in A at t and are in B at time $t + \tau$ lie in $\phi_{-\tau}(B) \cap A$. This is the wavy area in Figure 8. If we now assume that we have a probability measure η on X, one finds that the probability of the system being in B at time $t + \tau$ given that it was in A at t is $\eta(\phi_{-\tau}(B) \cap A)$.

No assumption about the nature of A and B has been made, and so we can take A to be a macro-region X_{M_i} and B to be another macro-region, X_{M_j}. The preceding formula then gives us the conditional probability that a system is in macro-state M_j at time $t + \tau$ given that it was in M_i at t. This prescription is completely general and can, in principle, be used in any version of BSM, including the ergodic approach and the RT account.

For the prescription to yield results, we have to specify what the measure η is. There are many options, but a particularly important one results from the approach to probability that we discussed at the end of the previous section, where we put a probability measure ξ over the initial macro-region of the system. With this in mind, we can introduce a measure on X through the rule $\eta(R) = \xi(\phi_{-t}(R))$, for all subsets R in X, where t is the total time that has elapsed since the process started at the initial time t_0. This has the important consequence that the measure of the area $\eta(\phi_{-\tau}(B) \cap A)$ at time t is given by the measure ξ over the initial macro-region. This allows us to state temporal conditional probabilities and calculate their values based on the probability distribution over the initial macro-region.

We can now return to Boltzmann's statement (in the quotation at the beginning of the section) that the system will steadily evolve towards more likely states until it reaches equilibrium. Recall that for Boltzmann the likelihood of a macro-state is proportional to the size of its macro-region and that the Boltzmann entropy is a monotonic function of the size of macro-regions. Having temporal conditional probabilities at hand, the statement can then be recast as the claim that for any non-equilibrium macro-state, the system is highly likely to evolve toward a higher-entropy macro-state in the future, until the system reaches equilibrium. This gives us the tendency that Boltzmann was after.

In this reading, Boltzmann makes a claim about conditional probabilities, specifically that the conditional probabilities for lower-to-higher entropy transitions are high (ideally close to one), while the probabilities for 'athermodynamical' transitions from higher-entropy to lower-entropy states are low (ideally close to zero). This raises the question whether the probabilities indeed work out in this way. We say more about it shortly. At this point we just note that this is in no way a given. Just as it depends on the nature of its dynamics whether a system behaves thermodynamically, it depends on its dynamics whether the conditional probabilities are such that lower-to-higher entropy transitions are highly likely.

If we now look back at the accounts we have discussed in this section, we notice that a conceptual question has arisen: what does it take to justify thermodynamic behaviour? There are different answers on the table. The ergodic account, the RT account, and the typicality account remain silent about the nature of the approach to equilibrium and only require that systems do approach equilibrium and spend most of their time in it. This is compatible with the approach to equilibrium exhibiting entropy fluctuations, and it does not imply a uniform progression from lower- to higher-entropy macro-states. By contrast, in the account that Boltzmann seems to endorse, the system is required to exhibit a *progression* from lower- to higher-entropy macro-states, which makes a monotonic increase of the Boltzmann entropy highly likely. This is a more stringent requirement than the requirement that a system must approach equilibrium and stay there most of the time. Which of these options is preferable is an interesting question for future research.

The challenge of explicating why transition probabilities for macro-states are such that a transition toward a higher-entropy macro-state is highly likely is a problem that is taken up in Albert's (2000) account of BSM. The key ingredient to address this challange is what Albert calls the *statistical postulate*, the posit that 'the right probability distribution to use for making inferences about the past and the future is the one that's uniform, on the standard measure, over those regions of phase space which are compatible with whatever other information – either in the form of laws or in the form of contingent empirical facts – we happen to have' (Albert 2000, 96). In formal terms this means that if we know that the state of a system is in set P and we want to know what the probability is that it is also in set Q, which is a subset of P, then the right probability is $\mu(Q)/\mu(P)$, where μ is the uniform measure.

Now focus on a macro-state M. Since every point lies on exactly one trajectory, we can separate the micro-states in X_M into those that evolve into a higher-entropy macro-state when they leave X_M and those that move into a lower-entropy macro-state when they leave X_M. Let us call these sets X_M^+ and X_M^- respectively. The statistical postulate then says that the probability of a system in M evolving toward a higher-entropy macro-state is $\mu(X_M^+)/\mu(X_M)$.

To make good on Boltzmann's tendency law, it would have to be the case that $\mu(X_M^+)/\mu(X_M)$ is high (ideally close to one) for all non-equilibrium macro-states. But now a nasty problem turns up. Due to the time-reversal invariance of the Hamiltonian dynamics, it is the case that whenever $\mu(X_M^+)/\mu(X_M)$ is high – and it is highly likely that the system will evolve into a higher-entropy macro-state in the future – it is also highly likely that the system has evolved into the current macro-state M from a macro-state of *higher* entropy. In other words, if the entropy is highly likely to increase in the future, it is also highly likely to have decreased in the past. This means that entropy has most likely decreased when the system moved into M, which contradicts the idea that a system evolves from a low-entropy condition to equilibrium.

Albert suggests solving this problem by taking the system under study to be the entire universe and then conditionalising on the so-called *past hypothesis*, the assumption 'that the world first came into being in whatever particular low-entropy highly condensed big-bang sort of macrocondition it is that the normal inferential procedures of cosmology will eventually present to us' (2000, 96). Let us call this state the *past state* M_p. If you look back at Figure 6 and assume that the system is the entire universe, then the past state would be X_{M_1} – the small macro-state in the lower left corner of the figure where the system starts its evolution.

To see how conditionalising on the past hypothesis solves the problem with a high-energy past, let us return to our discussion about conditional probabilities. As noted, we are free to pick A and B as we like. By assumption, the system was in the *past state* M_p when the universe came into being and it is in macro-state M now. So we know that the micro-state of the system at time t is in $I_t := \phi_t(X_{M_p}) \cap X_M$. Let this be our set A. What we want is that at a later time the system is in a macro-state of higher entropy. So let us define $\eta = \mu/\mu(I_t)$. Now choose B to be X_M^+, which we have introduced earlier. The conditional probability of a higher-entropy future then is $\eta(X_M^+ \cap I_t)$.[46] Albert argues that if we make the further (strong) assumption that 'abnormal' states – states with low-entropy futures – are scattered all over X_M, then a high-entropy future is highly likely. This is the desired result: as time evolves, transitions to states of higher entropy are highly likely while the system has a low-entropy past, as it should.

This approach to SM is based on three core elements: the deterministic time evolution of the system given by ϕ_t, the past hypothesis, and the statistical postulate. Together they result in the assignment of a probability to propositions about the history of a system. Albert (2015) calls this triad the *Mentaculus*. He regards the Mentaculus not only as an account of thermodynamic phenomena, but as the backbone of a complete scientific theory of the universe because the Mentaculus assigns probabilities to propositions in all sciences (and recall that the approach takes the system under investigation to be the entire universe).

---

[46] For a discussion of the technical aspects of the postulate, see Frigg (2010).

This raises all kind of issues about the nature of laws, reduction, and status of the special sciences, which we cannot cover in this Element.[47]

It is important to note that it is not a general fact about Hamiltonian systems that a high-entropy future is highly likely. As with other requirements concerning the evolution of systems, it will depend on the dynamics of the systems whether they hold. Albert's discussion proceeds under the assumption that systems of interest are such that they do provide the correct transition probabilities, but, as in other accounts, one would like to gain a better understanding of the dynamical conditions under which this is indeed the case. To the best of our knowledge, this question is largely unexplored, but an answer to it would be important to assess the merits of Albert's account.

Let us now comment on some further issues related to the Mentaculus. A crucial ingredient of the Mentaculus is the past hypothesis. The idea of grounding thermodynamic behaviour in a cosmic low-entropy past can be traced back to Boltzmann (Uffink 2007, 990) and has since been advocated by prominent physicists like Feynman (1965, ch. 5) and Penrose (2006, ch. 27). This raises two questions: first, can the past hypothesis be given a precise formulation that serves the purpose of SM, and, second, does the fact that the universe was created in this particular state require an explanation?

As regards the first question, Earman cast the damning verdict that the past hypothesis is 'not even false' (2006) because in cosmologies described in general relativity there is no well-defined sense in which the Boltzmann entropy has a low value. A further problem is that in the Mentaculus the Boltzmann entropy is a global quantity characterising the entire universe. But, as Winsberg points out, the fact that this quantity is low does not imply that the entropy of a particular small subsystem of interest is also low, and worse, just because the overall entropy of the universe increases it need not be the case that the entropy of a subsystem also increases (2004a). The source of these difficulties is that the Mentaculus takes the entire universe to be the relevant system. So one might try get around them by reverting to laboratory systems (like gases in a box) and then take the past state simply to be the state in which such a system is prepared at the beginning of a process. This leads to the so-called branch systems approach, which owes its name to the fact that a system is seen as 'branching off' from the rest of the universe when it is isolated from its environment and prepared in a non-equilibrium state (Davies 1974; Sklar 1993, 318–32). Albert (2000) dismisses this option for a number of reasons, chief among them that it is not

---

We refer the reader to Frisch (2011), Hemmo and Shenker (2022), and Myrvold et al. (2016) for discussions.

clear why one should regard the statistical postulate as valid for such a state (see Winsberg (2004b) for a discussion).

As regards the second question, Chen (2023), Goldstein (2001), and Loewer (2001) argue that past hypothesis has the status of a fundamental law of nature. Albert seems to regard it as something like a Kantian regulative principle in that its truth must be assumed in order to make knowledge of the past possible at all. By contrast, Callender and Price regard the past hypothesis as a contingent matter of fact, but they disagree on whether this fact stands in need of an explanation. Price (2004) argues that it does because the crucial question in SM is not why entropy increases but rather why it ever got to be low in the first place. Callender (2004) disagrees: the past hypothesis simply specifies initial conditions of a process, and initial conditions are not the kind of things that need to be explained (see also Sklar (1993, 309–18)). Parker (2005) argues that conditionalising on the initial state of the universe does not have the explanatory power to explain irreversible behaviour. Baras and Shenker (2020) and Farr (2022) analyse the notion of explanation that is involved in this debate and argue that different questions are in play that require different answers.

Another question that still needs to be settled is how the probabilities given by the formula $\mu(X_M^+ \cap I_t)/\mu(I_t)$ should be interpreted. As discussed in the previous section, to get a propensity interpretation off the ground one would need to work out a specific account showing how propensities can be consistent with determinism. Loewer (2001) suggested interpreting such probabilities as so-called *Humean objective chances* in Lewis' (1986) sense. Frigg (2008a, 2010) identifies some problems with this interpretation, and Frigg and Hoefer (2015) formulate an alternative Humean account that is designed to overcome these problems.[48]

3.9 Open Problems

BSM enjoys great popularity in foundational debates due to its clear and intuitive theoretical structure. Nevertheless, BSM faces a number of problems and limitations.

The first problem is that BSM only deals with closed systems that evolve under their own internal dynamics. As we will see in in the next section, GSM successfully deals with systems that can exchange energy and even particles with their environments, and systems of this kind play an important role in SM. Those who think that SM only deals with the entire universe can set this problem aside because the universe (arguably) is a closed system. However, those who think that the objects of study in SM are laboratory-size systems like

---

[48] For further discussion, see, for instance, Myrvold (2021).

gases and crystals will have to address the issues of how BSM can accommodate interactions between systems and their environments, which is a largely ignored problem.

A second problem is that even though macro-states are ubiquitous in discussions about BSM, little attention has been paid to a precise articulation of what these states are. There is loose talk about how a system looks from a macroscopic perspective, or there is a vague appeal to thermodynamic variables. However, by the lights of thermodynamics, variables like pressure and temperature are defined *only* in equilibrium and it remains unclear how non-equilibrium states, and with them the approach to equilibrium, should be characterised in terms of thermodynamic variables.[49] Frigg and Werndl (2023) suggest solving this problem by defining macro-states in terms of local field variables, but the issue needs further attention.

A third problem is that current formulations of BSM are closely tied to deterministic classical systems (Section 2). Some versions of BSM can be formulated based on classical stochastic systems (Werndl and Frigg 2017a). But the crucial question is whether, and if so how, a quantum version of BSM can be formulated. Dizadji-Bahmani (2011) discusses how a result due to Linden *et al.* (2009) can be used to construct an argument for the conclusion that an arbitrary small subsystem of a large quantum system typically tends towards equilibrium. Chen (2020) formulates a quantum version of the Mentaculus, which he calls the *Wentaculus*. These early steps have not yet resulted in a comprehensive and widely accepted formulation of a quantum version of BSM, and the formulation of such a version remains an understudied topic. Goldstein, Lebowitz, Tumulka, and Zanghì (2020) describe a quantum analogue of the Boltzmann entropy and argue that the Boltzmannian conception of equilibrium is vindicated also in quantum mechanics by recent work on the thermalisation of closed quantum systems. Albert (2000, ch. 7) suggested that the spontaneous collapses in the so-called GRW theory, a particular approach to quantum mechanics, could be responsible for the emergence of thermodynamic irreversibility. Te Vrug, Tóth, and Wittkowski (2021) put this proposal to test in computer simulations and found that GRW collapses do not always lead to thermodynamic behaviour and that therefore the GRW theory does not provide an explanation of irreversible behaviour.

A further question concerns phase transitions. As a matter of fact, phase transitions are usually discussed within GSM, and there is a question about how they can be understood and discussed in BSM. A natural definition would be

---

[49] A related issue is that temperature is always defined as kinetic energy, and this definition is stated for the ideal gas. There is a question as to whether this definition is cogent also for systems other than ideal gases.

that a phase transition occurs if an equilibrium value changes very rapidly in response to a change in an external parameter (or discontinuously if we consider an infinite limit). However, there is an interesting and underexplored question whether all important results about phase transitions that can be derived in the Gibbsian framework can be recovered from this definition.

Finally, there is no way around recognising that BSM is mostly used in foundational debates, but it is GSM that is the practitioner's workhorse. When physicists have to carry out calculations and solve problems, they usually turn to GSM, which offers user-friendly strategies that are often absent in BSM. So either BSM has to be extended with practical prescriptions, or it has to be connected to GSM so that it can benefit from its computational methods (for a brief discussion of the latter option see Section 4.8).

4 Gibbsian Statistical Mechanics

'Gibbsian Statistical Mechanics' is an umbrella term covering a number of positions that take Gibbs' (1902/1981) as their point of departure. In this section, we introduce the framework and discuss different versions and articulations of it, along with the issues they face.

The section is structured as follows. We begin by introducing the formalism of GSM and its most common interpretation, the ensemble interpretation (Section 4.1). The Averaging Principle plays an important role in GSM. Yet there are questions about how exactly this principle should be articulated. A classical albeit unsuccessful articulation is based on ergodicity (Section 4.2). Probabilism offers an alternative interpretation of the formalism of GSM (Section 4.3). Assuming probabilism, an articulation of the Averaging Principle in terms of fluctuations being small can be given (Section 4.4). Understanding the approach to equilibrium in GSM faces two main obstacles: that the entropy is a constant of motion and that equilibrium is defined in terms of stationarity (Section 4.5). A traditional way to get around these difficulties is to introduce a coarse-graining on the state space (Section 4.6). An alternative solution is to give up the assumption that systems are isolated and see the approach to equilibrium as the result of outside influences on the system (Section 4.7). The epistemic account interprets SM not as a description of mind-independent systems but as an account of our state of knowledge about them (Section 4.8). There is an important question about how to understand the relation between GSM and BSM, and different proposals have been made (Section 4.9). We end by summarising open problems for GSM (Section 4.10).

Philosophy of Physics

4.1 A Primer on GSM

Like BSM, GSM starts with the dynamical system (X, ϕ_t, μ) introduced in Section 2.1. But this is where the commonalities end. Rather than partitioning the phase space into macro-regions, GSM starts by introducing probabilities. In Section 2.6 we introduced the formal apparatus of probability theory, and in Section 2.7 we saw that one of the points of contact between probability theory and mechanics is that the mechanical state space X can serve as the event space Ω of probability theory. This is exactly what happens in GSM, which puts a probability density function, often referred to as a 'distribution', on X. In principle the probability density function can depend on time, and to make this dependence explicit we write $\rho_t(x)$.

Since $\rho_t(x)$ is a probability on X, it follows immediately that the probability at time t of a region R in X is

$$p_t(R) = \int_R \rho_t(x) \, dx, \tag{5}$$

where the 'R' below the integration sign indicates that we are integrating over R.

The distribution evolves under the dynamics of the system through the law $\rho_t(x) = \rho_0(\phi_{-t}(x))$ where ρ_0 is the distribution at the initial time t_0 and $\phi_{-t}(x)$ is the micro-state that evolves into x after time t. If we trace R's time evolution, $R_t := \phi_t(R)$, then $p_t(R_t)$ is the same for all t: $dp_t(R_t)/dt = 0$.[50]

At the macro-level, a system is characterised by macro-variables, which are functions $f : X \to \mathbb{R}$, where $\mathbb{R}$ are the real numbers. With the exception of entropy and temperature (to which we turn in the following discussion), GSM takes all physical quantities to be represented by such functions. The so-called *phase average* of f is

$$\langle f \rangle = \int_X f(x)\rho_t(x)dx, \tag{6}$$

where the integration is over the entire state space X.[51]

GSM also introduces a notion of entropy, now known as the *Gibbs entropy*:

$$S_G = -k_B \int_X \rho_t(x)\log[\rho_t(x)]dx, \tag{7}$$

which is a property of the probability density function $\rho_t(x)$.

---

[50] It can be proven that this is the case if and only if the so-called Liouville equation is satisfied.

[51] The term 'phase average' is owed to the fact that, as noted in Section 2.2, the state space of a Hamiltonian system is also known as the 'phase space'. 'State space average' would be a better term, but since 'phase average' is common in the literature, we stick with it.

A distribution is called *stationary* if it does not change over time, that is, $\rho_t(x) = \rho_0(x)$ for all t. If the distribution is stationary, Gibbs says that the system is in 'statistical equilibrium' (1902/1981, 6). If a system is in statistical equilibrium, then $\langle f \rangle$ does not depend on time. Stationarity is therefore what defines equilibrium in GSM. In this case we simplify notation and only write $\rho(x)$. We note, and this will be important later on, that Gibbs' statistical equilibrium is a condition on a probability distribution and *not* on a physical system per se.

It is a simple result in Hamiltonian dynamics that a distribution that is a function *only* of the Hamiltonian H is stationary and therefore an equilibrium distribution. That is, all distributions of the form $\rho(x) = \rho(H(x))$ are equilibrium distributions. This is a very large class of distributions, and there is a question about which of these characterise physically relevant situations. Gibbs discusses this problem at length and formulates three distributions which are still used today: the *microcanonical distribution* for isolated systems, the *canonical distribution* for systems with fluctuating energy, and the *grand-canonical distribution* for systems with both fluctuating energy and fluctuating particle number. Since nothing in what follows depends on the exact form of these distributions, we will not state them here. For formal definitions of these distributions, see, for instance, Tolman (1938/1979) and Lavis (2015), and for philosophical discussions, see Davey (2008, 2009) and Myrvold (2016).

So far, our discussion has been couched in purely formal terms. But if GSM is to be a theory of physical systems rather than a piece of mathematics, it must be interpreted in physical terms. This requires, first, that we interpret $\rho_t(x)$ in one of the ways outlined in Section 2.6 and, second, that we say what the empirical predictions of the theory are. As we will see, these problems are closely related, and a response to one has implications for a response to the other.

Let us start with $\rho_t(x)$. As we have seen in Section 2.6, once probabilities are introduced mathematically through the axioms of probability, they must be interpreted in terms of something non-mathematical to connect the formal apparatus to a domain of scientific investigation, with relative frequencies, propensities, and the codification of ignorance being the most common interpretations. In the context of GSM, the question of interpretation is fraught with difficulties. We will discuss these difficulties at length in later sections, but before doing so it is worth introducing Gibbs' own answer in some detail because it still is the preferred interpretation in many textbooks, and it provides the backdrop against which contemporary discussions are conducted.

Gibbs answers the question of interpretation in terms of an *ensemble*, which he introduces thus: 'Let us imagine a great number of independent systems, identical in nature, but differing in phase, that is, in their condition with respect to configuration and velocity. The forces are supposed to be determined for every system by the same law, being functions of the coördinates of the system' (1902/1981, 5).

Hence, an ensemble is an imaginary collection of systems of the kind we are interested in, or, as Schrödinger puts it, a collection of 'mental copies of the one system under consideration' (1952/1989, 3). It is crucial not to conflate an ensemble with a collection of micro constituents of a system. Of course, one could say that a gas is an ensemble of molecules. But that is not the intended meaning of 'ensemble' in GSM. An ensemble, as introduced by Gibbs, is a collection of imaginary copies of the *entire* gas, not a collection of molecules. Hence, ensembles are not physical objects: ensembles have no spatiotemporal existence, and there is no physical interaction between members of an ensemble.

The systems in the ensemble have the same state space X and the same time evolution ϕ_t, but they can differ in their state x at a given time t. Since an ensemble is a collection of systems, one can ask 'how many' systems there are in a certain part of X. The distribution $\rho_t(x)$ can be seen as providing an answer to this question because it can be interpreted as encoding what proportion of systems in the ensemble are in states that are located in a certain subset of X. In formal terms, we can then interpret the integral in the right-hand side of Equation (5) as the fraction of systems in the ensemble whose state is in R at time t. If, for instance, the value of the integral is 0.6 at time t, this means that at that time 60 per cent of the systems in the ensemble are in a state that lies in R. In this way $\rho_t(x)$ can be seen as describing the ensemble, and for this reason the averages defined in Equation (6) are then referred to as 'ensemble averages'.

If, as a next step, one also adopts some sort of frequency interpretation of probability, this fraction translates into a probability: if the fraction of systems in R is y, then the probability of finding a randomly chosen system in R is y. The idea here is that an ensemble is like an urn with balls of different colours. If, say, 35 per cent of the balls in the urn are red, then in a long sequence of random draws from the urn we will find that the relative frequency of red balls is 0.35, and therefore the probability of drawing a red ball is 0.35. Gibbs explicitly endorses such an interpretation when he comments that '[w]hat we know about a body can generally be described most accurately and most simply by saying that it is one taken at random from a great number (ensemble) of bodies which are completely described' (Gibbs 1902/1981, 163).[52]

Gibbs' condition of 'statistical equilibrium' is then a condition on the state of the ensemble which says that the ensemble is in equilibrium if the probabilities for certain events do not change. Hence, equilibrium now appears as a property of an ensemble rather than of an individual system. This is a curious shift. We set out to understand how systems – physical objects like gases in containers – behave, and we end up talking about ensembles – imaginary collections of mental copies of such systems. These are obviously different things and so at the very least, there is a question about how the study of ensembles bears on the study of systems. In particular, what do calculations performed on an ensemble tell us about the properties of a system? Or, put in terms of experiments, what do ensemble calculations tell us about experimental results?

This brings us to the second question for GSM, namely what the empirical predictions of the theory are. A standard answer appeals to averaging. In their textbook on SM, Pathria and Beale formulate the position as follows: '*the ensemble average of any physical quantity f is identical to the value one expects to obtain on making an appropriate measurement on the given system*' (Pathria and Beale 2011, 31, original italics), and they call this the 'most important result' in SM (ibid.). The practice of calculating averages and associating them with measurement outcomes is also called *phase averaging*. Prescriptions like Pathria and Beale's are common in the literature on GSM, although different authors give different formulations of the prescription, and they add different qualifications and restrictions.[53] We will discuss some of these in later sections. Such a discussion is aided by having a general formulation of the prescription. This formulation is what we call the *Averaging Principle* (AP): under condition C, when measuring the physical quantity represented by function f on a system in thermal equilibrium, the observed equilibrium value of the property is expected to be the average $\langle f \rangle$ of an ensemble in ensemble-equilibrium.

The content of this principle is underdetermined in three ways. First, 'condition C' is a placeholder and a full specification of C will have to be given. Second, since the principle appeals to measurements, a theory of measurement will have to be supplied. Third, what does it mean for results to be 'expected'? Resolving these underdeterminations amounts to offering an *articulation* of the principle. As we will see, different schools of thought offer different articulations, and as of yet there is no universally accepted version of AP.

<hr>

[52] Gibbs is no exception. This interpretation is repeated in many textbooks. For references, see Frigg and Werndl (2021, 121–2).

[53] For extensive references to textbooks on this matter, see Frigg and Werndl (2021, 109–10).

Filling these gaps is a significant task, but notice that they add up to only half of the issues that GSM faces. In Section 1.1 we said that the core task for SM is to characterise the state of equilibrium and to account for why, and how, a system approaches equilibrium. So far we have only dealt with equilibrium, and how to conceptualise non-equilibrium in GSM is still an open question. We turn to this issue in Sections 4.5 to 4.8.

At the end of Section 3 we noted that the lack of a quantum version of BSM is a significant lacuna. GSM does not face this problem. In fact, there is a well-developed quantum version of GSM that is a cornerstone of the practice of the discipline. Space constraints prevent us from discussing it in this introduction, but we emphasise that GSM is successful in the quantum domain.[54]

4.2 Articulating AP: Ergodicity

The averaging principle says that under condition C the outcome of a measurement of a property f on a system in equilibrium is expected to be $\langle f \rangle$. What are the conditions, what does it mean to measure property f, and in what sense exactly should we expect the measured value to be $\langle f \rangle$? The standard textbook answer invokes ergodicity (which we have introduced in Section 2.5) and runs as follows.[55] Carrying out a measurement of f takes time, and hence what the measurement device registers is the time average of f over the duration of the measurement. So the measurement outcome is a finite time average. However, the time that it takes to perform a measurement is long compared to the time scale on which typical molecular processes take place, and for this reason the finite time average of the measurement is approximately equal to the *infinite* time average of the measured function. As we have seen, in an ergodic system infinite time averages are equal to phase averages (for almost all initial conditions). If one now assumes that the system is ergodic, one can equate the time average and the ensemble average. This provides the sought-after articulation of AP: C is being ergodic; to perform a measurement of property f means to keep a device that is set up to measure f in contact with the system for long enough to register a time average of f; and the expectation is universal because the measured value is always equal to $\langle f \rangle$.

In this articulation, the principle fails for a number of reasons. First, as Malament and Zabell (1980, 342–3) and Sklar (1993, 176–9) point out, from the fact that measurements take time it does not follow that what is measured are time averages. So the association of measurement results with time averages is

---

[54] For an exposition of the theory, see, for instance, Tolman (1938/1979); for a philosophical discussion of quantum SM, see Emch (2007).

[55] See, for instance, Chandler (1987, 57–9), and for further references, see Frigg and Werndl (2021, 111).

unjustified. And even if one could somehow argue that measurement devices output time averages, equating these *finite* averages with *infinite* time averages is problematic because finite and infinite averages can assume very different values even if the duration of the finite measurement is long compared to the time scale on which molecular processes take place. Second, this account makes a mystery of why we observe change. As we have seen in Section 1.1, we do observe systems approaching equilibrium, and in doing so we observe macro-variables changing their values. In the example with the gas, we will observe the volume and the pressure of the gas change. If measurements produced infinite time averages, then no change would ever be observed because infinite averages are constant by definition. Third, as we already noted in Section 3.3, ergodicity is a stringent condition and many systems to which SM is successfully applied are not ergodic. But if a system is not ergodic, time averages do not have to be equal to phase averages, which pulls the rug from underneath the proposed justification of AP.

A number of approaches have been developed to either solve or circumvent these problems.[56] Malament and Zabell (1980) suggest a method of justifying phase averaging that still invokes ergodicity but avoids an appeal to time averages. Vranas (1998) offers a reformulation of this argument for systems that are epsilon-ergodic (see Section 3.3). This accounts for systems that are 'almost' ergodic, but it remains silent about systems that are far from ergodic. Khinchin (1949/1960) restricts attention to systems with a large number of degrees of freedom and so-called sum functions (i.e. functions that are a sum over one-particle functions), and he shows that for such systems $f^* = \langle f \rangle$ holds on the largest part of X. However, as Khinchin himself notes, the focus on sum-functions is too restrictive to cover realistic systems, and the approach also reverts to the implausible posit that observations yield infinite time averages.

4.3 Probabilism

Probabilism submits that the discussion has taken a wrong turn right at the start. Gibbsian SM, so the argument goes, is not a theory about phase averages but about probabilities. The core of GSM is the normalised measure $\rho_t(x)$, which gives the probabilities for events to occur, and so this measure must be the centrepiece of any analysis of GSM.[57]

---

[56] For want of space, we cannot discuss these approaches in any detail. For a more extensive discussion, see Frigg (2008b, 146–55) and references therein.

[57] Probabilism has an odd status. On the one hand it seems to be a widely held view in the foundations of physics community, and it has been suggested to us as the correct interpretation of GSM on numerous occasions. On the other hand, explicit statements of it in the literature are few and far between.

Probabilism is based on two core assumptions. The first assumption is that $\rho_t(x)$ gives the correct probabilities for *all events* to occur at *all times*. This is a natural assumption in GSM because it effectively means that Equation (5) is valid without restrictions, which has been tacitly assumed in Section 4.1. The second assumption concerns the nature of measurements. In a radical break with the ergodic approach in the previous section, probabilism adopts the notion of an *instantaneous measurement*, which sees a measurement as happening at a particular instant of time. Penrose describes a measurement of that kind as 'an instantaneous act, like taking a snapshot' (1970, 17–18). This amounts to saying that if a measurement of a physical quantity represented by f is performed on a system at time t and the micro-state of the system at time t is x, then the measurement outcome will be $f(x)$. An obvious consequence of this definition is that measurements at different times can have different outcomes, and the values of macro-variables can change over time.

Following Wallace (2015), one can then insist that the quantitative content of statistical mechanics is exhausted by the statistics of observables (their expectation values, variances, etc.), which follow from $\rho_t(x)$. GSM is a probabilistic theory that characterises a system's statistical equilibrium and specifies how likely a system will be found in certain micro-states – and that is all that there is to GSM.[58]

While the posit that measurements are snapshots of the kind described seems plausible (or at least a good approximation to what happens in actual measurements), the assumption that Equation (5) is universally valid cannot be quite right. Assume that $\rho_t(x)$ is one of the standard stationary equilibrium distributions such as the microcanonical distribution, which is uniform on the energy hypersurface.[59] Now track the behaviour of the system over time (one considers the limit as time goes to infinity), when the system starts in a particular initial condition x at time t_0 and its state evolves under ϕ_t. Under this interpretation probabilism then asserts that for all $R \subset X$ and all times t, Equation (5) gives the

---

[58] McCoy (2020) provides an explicit articulation of this view in which $\rho_t(x)$ is interpreted as the system's state rather than as a probability distribution over states. For a discussion, see Frigg and Werndl (2021, sec. 5).

[59] An anonymous referee has drawn our attention to an alternative approach. The approach begins with ρ_0 and interprets it as the measurement uncertainty of the initial state. Accordingly, $\rho_t(x)$ is the initial uncertainty moved forward in time. Equation (5) is then universally valid *with respect to the uncertainty about the system's initial condition*. With this $\rho_t(x)$, one can calculate averages which are correct *in that sense*. This is an interesting suggestion that deserves further attention. The view is not without problems, though. While one can write down an equation of motion for $\rho_t(x)$, one cannot in general solve this equation and hence one does not know the precise shape of $\rho_t(x)$. But without an explicit statement of $\rho_t(x)$, this view is useless in practice. Furthermore, the view lacks a connection to the standard practice in GSM of calculating phase averages w.r.t. the stationary measure, and hence, under this view, this standard practice remains mysterious.

correct values of the long-run fraction of time that $x(t)$ is in R as time goes to infinity. Under this interpretation, without further qualification, it cannot be right that (5) holds.

To see why, consider the situation shown in Figure 3 and assume that what you see in the figure is the energy hypersurface (and so the distribution is uniform over the surface). In Section 2.2 we have seen that trajectories cannot cross invariant surfaces. But the invariant surface divides X roughly in the middle and so according to Equation (5) the probability of finding the system to the left of the invariant surface is about ½, and ditto for the probability of finding the system to the right of the invariant surface. But this is wrong. If the initial condition of the system lies, say, in the part of X that is to the right of the invariant surface, then the system will *never* cross over to the part to the left of the invariant surface. So the probability of finding the system in the left half should be zero, not ½.

One way of avoiding these difficulties is to require that the dynamics of the system be such that it can access all parts of X. In deterministic systems this is tantamount to requiring that the system be ergodic. Some systems are of this kind: for all we know the hard ball gas is ergodic. But as we have already noted on several occasions, many SM systems are not ergodic, and so this is not a general solution to the problem.

But maybe requiring systems to be ergodic is asking for too much. All that is needed is that a system being trapped in a certain invariant subset of X (like the set on the left of the invariant surface in Figure 3) does not influence the probabilities of measurements of macroscopic quantities given by a function f. This happens if the proportion of states (relative to $\rho_t(x)$) for which f assumes a particular value is the same in each invariant subset as it is in the entire state space. In this case, the probabilities one would get if one calculated them in the invariant subset of X in which the system is trapped are identical to the probabilities one would get if one calculated them for the entire X. In other words, what we need is that invariant sets of the dynamics (if any) and the function f harmonise with each other so as to 'mask' the fact that the system is trapped in certain invariant sets. We call this the *masking condition.*

Under what circumstances does the masking condition hold? As far as we can see, there are no general criteria to decide whether a system has this property. In fact, whether a trapping will be masked in this way depends on both the time evolution $\phi_t(x)$ and the function f, and so one will have to look at each $f-\phi_t(x)$ pair to come to a verdict. A positive result cannot be taken for granted. If a system is not ergodic, there will always be functions f for which the masking condition fails.

Have we got carried away by dynamical systems theory? To see whether we have, let us consider yet another interpretation of the probabilities in Equation (5). In Section 4.1 we introduced ensembles, and if we think about GSM probabilities as ensemble probabilities (which, recall, are like drawing balls from of an urn), then none of these problems arise because subsequent draws are independent and hence are not constrained by invariant surfaces in the state space. Indeed, Gibbs seems to reject a dynamical systems way of thinking explicitly when he introduces ensemble methods by observing that '[w]e may imagine a great number of systems of the same nature [. . .] And here we may set the problem, not to follow a particular system through its succession of config-urations, but to determine how the whole number of systems will be distributed among the various conceivable configurations and velocities at any required time [. . .]' (Gibbs 1902/1981, p. vii).

When put forward without further qualifications, it is difficult to see how this captures a realistic physical situation. What we have in front of us in a labora-tory situation is a particular system, and this system has an initial condition x which evolves under the time evolution of the system and thereby traces the trajectory $\phi_t(x)$. This means that states at different times are highly correlated. Hence, as long as one maintains that, at bottom, an SM system is a triple (X, ϕ_t, μ), one cannot also maintain that a system behaves like balls randomly drawn from an urn.

'Without further qualifications' is crucial. One could argue that while subsequent observations on the same system are in general not independent, SM systems fall into a special class of system for which (at least approximate) independence holds. In this vein, Kittel argues that 'the complex systems with which we are dealing appear to randomise themselves between observations, provided only that the observations follow each other by a time interval longer than a certain characteristic time called the relaxation time' (Kittel 1958/2004, 7). This is too strong because randomisation in a finite time span between observations is typically impossible.[60] So one might try to relax the requirement and only demand that correlations relax below a level where they become negligible. One can show that in general approximate re-randomisation after a sufficiently long time requires a system to have a property called *mixing* (we discuss mixing briefly in Section 4.6). But since mixing is strictly stronger than ergodicity (i.e. mixing implies ergodicity but not vice versa), this is a non-starter for all the reasons we have already seen.

Yet, requiring approximate re-randomisation may well be too much because all we really need is that subsequent f-measurements are independent. If this is

---

[60] Indeed, complete independence can only ever be reached for certain partitions and only for Bernoulli systems.

the case, we say that a system exhibits f-independence. The question then is: when do systems exhibit f-independence? As with the masking condition, the answer is that it depends and that one has to look at each triple consisting of f, $\phi_t(x)$, and the elapsed time period t, to come to a verdict.

The conclusion is that if measurements are 'snapshots' in the sense described at the beginning of this section, then the probability for certain outcomes is given by $\rho_t(x)$ through Equation (5) only if additional conditions like the masking condition or f-independence hold. Neither condition is trivial,[61] and so there is a question of the circumstances under which they apply. We expect that these conditions hold in some but not all situations in which one would like to apply GSM. More has to be said about the circumstances under which the conditions hold.

4.4 Articulating AP: Fluctuations

Probabilism does not include AP. But probabilism can be used to provide an articulation of AP by appealing to fluctuations.[62] Let us assume, with probabilism, that measurements are snapshots and that we are in a situation in which Equation (5) gives the correct probabilities. The probability of obtaining a certain value F when performing a measurement of a quantity represented by function f is then equal to the probability of the micro-state of the system being in region R_F, the region of all x for which $f(x) = F$. This probability is given by Equation (5) if we integrate over R_F. We can now choose $F = \langle f \rangle$, and the probability of the measurement outcome being the phase average is then the integral over $R_{\langle f \rangle}$. What is more, we can also calculate the probabilities of fluctuations away from $\langle f \rangle$. By definition, a *fluctuation* $\Delta(t)$ is the difference between $\langle f \rangle$ and the instantaneous value of f at time t:

$$\Delta(t) = f(x(t)) - \langle f \rangle,$$

and we call the absolute value of $\Delta(t)$, $|\Delta(t)|$, the *magnitude* of the fluctuation. We can now again use Equation (5) to calculate the probability of a fluctuation of a certain magnitude. Specifically, let us consider a fluctuation whose magnitude lies between two values δ_1 and δ_2 (where $0 \leq \delta_1 \leq \delta_2$). The probability of such a fluctuation is, again, given by Equation (5) if we integrate over R_D, where $D = \{x \in X \mid \delta_1 \leq |\Delta(t)| \leq \delta_2\}$.

---

[61] For examples of systems in which the conditions fail, see Frigg and Werndl (2021, 124–5).

[62] Fluctuations are occasionally mentioned in SM books in connection with AP (see, for instance, Hill (1956/1987) and Schrödinger (1952/1989)), and it has often been proposed to us in conversation as the correct justification of AP. This section is an attempt to give an explicit statement of a fluctuation interpretation of GSM based on Frigg and Werndl (2021).

Intuitively one expects the probability of finding $\langle f \rangle$ as the measurement outcome to be very high, and the fluctuations to be such that only small fluctuations are likely while medium and large fluctuations are highly unlikely. A system that exhibits this pattern approximately mimics thermodynamic behaviour, so we refer to fluctuations that have these characteristics as *thermodynamic fluctuations*. $\langle f \rangle$ is then the expected measurement outcome in the sense that the probability of $R_{\langle f \rangle}$ is very high (indeed, very close to one) and hence the probability of $R_{\neg \langle f \rangle}$ is low (where '$\neg$' is the negation). In this vein, Hill submits that the validity of the identification of observed values with ensemble averages is legitimate only when the fluctuations of f away from $\langle f \rangle$ are small (Hill 1956/1987, 9–10) and Schrödinger declares '[m]ean value, most probable value, any values that occur with non-vanishing probability – all become the same thing' (1952/1989, 35).

As we have seen, AP says that under condition C the outcome of a measurement of a property f on a system in equilibrium is expected to be $\langle f \rangle$. The fluctuation account articulates the blanks in the principle as follows: measurements are snapshots (in the sense introduced in Section 4.3); we expect a measurement outcome to be $\langle f \rangle$ in the sense that the probability of $R_{\langle f \rangle}$ is high; and C is the condition that fluctuations in the system are thermodynamic.

That fluctuations are thermodynamic cannot be taken for granted. While the fluctuations in many GSM systems turn out to be thermodynamic as expected, there are important systems studied in SM in which this is not the case.[63] Ultimately, whether fluctuations are thermodynamic depends on the choice of $\rho_t(x)$, the dynamics of the system, and the function f. At this point, we would like to have a theorem that states under what conditions a system has thermodynamic fluctuations. To the best of our knowledge, no general theorem of this kind is currently available.[64]

4.5 GSM and the Approach to Equilibrium

So far, we have focused on the characterisation of equilibrium in GSM, and in practice GSM is mostly used as an equilibrium theory. However, to be a comprehensive theory, GSM must also account for the approach to equilibrium. The approach to equilibrium is often characterised through an increase of

---

[63] For instance, fluctuations in the Kac ring with the standard macro-state structure of the number of black and white balls as discussed by Lavis (2008) are not thermodynamic, and neither are fluctuations in the baker's gas with a function f that takes integer values on cells of the standard Boltzmannian partition (Werndl and Frigg 2017b).

[64] There is, however, a powerful result that applies to a large class of cases: if the probability of finding the system in R is given through Equation (5) and if the so-called Khinchin Condition holds, then the system exhibits thermodynamic fluctuations. For a discussion of the Khinchin Condition, see Section 4.9 and Werndl and Frigg (2020b, sec. 4).

entropy. So, one might say that GSM can help itself to this characterisation and posit that in an approach to equilibrium the Gibbs entropy S_G (introduced in Section 4.1) increases until it reaches its maximum.

Unfortunately, this idea is undercut immediately by a mathematical theorem saying that S_G is a constant of motion: $S_G[\rho_t(x)] = S_G[\rho_0(x)]$ for all time t. Hence, not only does S_G fail to increase monotonically; it does not change at all! This precludes a characterisation of the approach to equilibrium in terms of increasing Gibbs entropy. Hence, either such a characterisation must be abandoned, or the formalism has to be modified to allow S_G to increase.

A second problem is a consequence of the Gibbsian definition of statistical equilibrium. As we have seen in Section 4.1, a system is in statistical equilibrium if $\rho_t(x)$ is stationary. A system away from equilibrium would then have to be associated with a non-stationary distribution and eventually evolve into the stationary equilibrium distribution. But this is mathematically impossible. It is a consequence of the formalism of the theory of GSM that a distribution that is stationary at some point in time has to be stationary at all times (past and future), and that a distribution that is non-stationary at some point in time will always be non-stationary. Hence $\rho_t(x)$ cannot evolve from a non-stationary distribution to a stationary distribution. This requires either a change in the definition of equilibrium, or a change in the formalism that would allow distributions to change in the requisite way.[65] In what follows we discuss the main attempts to address these problems.[66]

4.6 Coarse-Graining

Gibbs was aware of the problems with the approach to equilibrium and proposed coarse-graining as a solution (Gibbs 1902/1981, ch. 12). This notion has since been endorsed by many practitioners.[67] We have already encountered coarse-graining in Section 4.2. The use of it here is slightly different, though, because we are now putting a grid on the full state space X and not just on the one-particle space. One can then define a coarse-grained density $\bar{\rho}_t(x)$ by saying that at every point x in X the value of $\bar{\rho}_t(x)$ is the average of $\rho_t(x)$ over the grid cell in which x lies. The advantage of coarse-graining is that the coarse-grained distribution is not subject to the same limitations as the original distribution. Specifically, let us call the Gibbs entropy that is calculated with the coarse-grained distribution the *coarse-grained Gibbs entropy*. It turns out that the

---

[65] An interesting change would be to replace being stationarity by being *forward stationary*, the requirement that a distribution does not change any more from a certain instant of time onward.

[66] For a brief discussion of alternative approaches that we cannot cover here, see Frigg (2008b, 166–8) and references therein.

[67] See, for instance, Farquhar (1964) and Penrose (1970).

coarse-grained Gibbs entropy is not a constant of motion, and it is possible for the entropy to increase. This re-opens the avenue of understanding the approach to equilibrium in terms of an increase of entropy. It is also possible for the coarse-grained distribution to evolve so that it spreads out evenly over the entire available space and thereby comes to look like a micro-canonical equilibrium distribution. Such a distribution is also known as the quasi-equilibrium distribution (Blatt 1959; Ridderbos 2002).

Coarse-graining raises two questions. First, the coarse-grained entropy *can* increase and the system *can* approach a coarse-grained equilibrium, but under what circumstances will they actually do so? Second, is it legitimate to replace standard equilibrium by quasi-equilibrium?

As regards the first question, the standard answer (which also goes back to Gibbs) is that the system has to be *mixing*. Intuitively speaking, a system is mixing if every subset of X ends up being spread out evenly over the entire state space in the long run.[68] The problem with this is that, as we have already noted in Section 4.3, mixing is a demanding condition because mixing implies ergodicity. And even if a system is mixing, the mixed state is only achieved in the limit for $t \to \infty$, but real physical systems reach equilibrium in finite time.

As regards the second question, the motivation for adopting quasi-equilibrium is that $\bar{\rho}_t(x)$ and $\rho_t(x)$ are taken to be empirically indistinguishable. If the size of the grid is below the measurement precision, then no measurement will be able to tell the difference between the two. Hence, there is no reason to prefer $\rho_t(x)$ to $\bar{\rho}_t(x)$. This premise has been challenged. Blatt (1959) and Ridderbos and Redhead (1998) argue that this is wrong because the spin-echo experiment (Hahn 1950) makes it possible to empirically discern between $\rho_t(x)$ and $\bar{\rho}_t(x)$. The weight of this experiment continues to be discussed controversially, with some authors insisting that it invalidates the coarse-graining approach (Ridderbos 2002) and others insisting that coarse-graining can still be defended (Ainsworth 2005; Lavis 2004; Robertson 2020).[69]

4.7 Interventionism

The approaches we discussed so far assume that systems are isolated. This is an idealising assumption because real physical systems are not perfectly isolated from their environments. This is the starting point for *interventionism*,

---

[68] For an introductory characterisation of mixing, see Berkovitz, Frigg, and Kronz (2011).

[69] We also note that a silent conceptual shift has occurred when introducing the coarse-grained distribution: Gibbs defined equilibrium through stationarity, while the coarse-graining approach defines it through uniformity. This needs further justification, but in principle there would seem to be nothing to stop us from redefining equilibrium in this way.

which is based on the idea that real systems are constantly subject to outside perturbations, and that the system is Driven to equilibrium through these perturbations. This position has been formulated by Blatt (1959) and further developed by Ridderbos and Redhead (1998). The key insight behind the approach is that the two challenges introduced in Section 4.3 vanish once the system is not assumed to be isolated: the entropy can increase, and a non-stationary distribution can be pushed towards a distribution that is stationary in the future.

This approach accepts that isolated systems do not approach equilibrium, and one may wonder why this would be the case. If one places a gas of the kind that we discussed in Section 1 somewhere in interstellar space where it is isolated from outside influences, would it really not approach equilibrium? And even if this were the case, would adding just *any* environment resolve the issue? Environments can be of very different kinds and there is no general theorem that says that any environment drives a system to equilibrium. Indeed, there are reasons to assume that there is no such theorem because while environments do drive systems, they need not drive them to equilibrium. It remains an unresolved question under what conditions environments drive systems to equilibrium.

Another challenge for interventionism is that one is always free to consider a larger system consisting of the original system plus its environment. For instance, we can consider the 'gas + box' system. This system would then also approach equilibrium because of outside influences, and we can then again form an even larger system, for instance the 'gas + box + laboratory' system. So, we get into a regress that only ends once the system under study is the entire universe. But the universe has no environment that could serve as a source of perturbations, which, so the criticism goes, shows that the programme fails.

Whether one sees this criticism as decisive depends on one's views of laws of nature. The argument relies on the premise that the underlying theory is a universal theory, namely one that applies to everything that there is without restrictions. But while universality is widely held, some have argued against it because laws are always tested in highly artificial situations. Claiming that they equally apply outside these settings involves a problematic inductive leap; see, for instance, Cartwright (1999) for a discussion of such a view. This, if true, might undercut the preceding argument against interventionism, but a lot will depend on how exactly the scope of laws is understood.

These are serious issues, and we take it that the burden of proof lies on interventionists to show that these issues can be resolved.

4.8 The Epistemic Account

The epistemic account urges a radical reconceptualisation of SM. The account goes back to Tolman (1938/1979) and has been brought to prominence by Jaynes in a string of publications between 1955 and 1980, most of which are gathered in Jaynes (1983). In Section 2.6 we have seen that there are three major interpretations of probability: frequencies, propensities, and credences. In Sections 4.1 and 4.3 we encountered frequency interpretations of $\rho_t(x)$; the epistemic account is based on an ignorance interpretation of $\rho_t(x)$.[70] On this approach, SM is about our *knowledge* of the world and not about the world itself, and the probability distributions in GSM represent our state of knowledge rather than mind-independent matters of fact. The centrepiece of this interpretation is the fact that the Gibbs entropy is formally identical to the Shannon entropy in information theory, which is a measure for the lack of information about a system: the higher the entropy, the less we know.[71] The Gibbs entropy can therefore be seen as quantifying our lack of information about a system. This has the advantage that ensembles are no longer needed in the statement of GSM. On the epistemic account, there is only one system, the one on which we are performing our experiments, and $\rho_t(x)$ codifies what we know about it. This also offers a natural criterion for identifying equilibrium distributions: they are the distributions with the highest entropy consistent with the external constraints on the system because such distributions are the least committal distributions. This is known as Jaynes' *maximum entropy principle.*

The maximum entropy principle has been discussed controversially, and, to date, there is no consensus on its significance, or even cogency.[72] A further concern is that the dynamics of the system plays no role in the epistemic approach. This is problematic for the reasons we have seen in Section 4.3: if the dynamics has invariant quantities, a system cannot access certain parts of the state space even though $\rho_t(x)$ may assign a non-zero probability to it (Sklar 1993, 193–4).

The explanation of the epistemic account of the approach to equilibrium relies on making repeated measurements and conditionalising on each measurement result; for a discussion, see Sklar (1993, 255–7). This successfully gets

---

[70] Propensity interpretations have been less prominent in the discussion of GSM, but they do exist. McCoy (2020) presents an interpretation of GSM according to which $\rho_t(x)$ is the state of the system, where this state specifies the 'potentialities' of the system. Space constraints prevent us from getting deeper into this here. For a discussion of McCoy's approach, see Frigg and Werndl (2021, 112–16).

[71] For an introductory discussion of information theory and Shannon's entropy, see Adriaans (2020).

[72] For discussion, see, for instance, Howson and Urbach (2006), Uffink (1995, 1996a), and Williamson (2010).

around the problem that the Gibbs entropy is constant because the value assignments now depend not only on the system's internal dynamics but also on the action of an experimenter. The problem with this solution is that depending on how exactly the calculations are done, either the entropy increase fails to be monotonic (indeed entropy decreases are possible) or the entropy curve will become dependent on the sequence of instants of time chosen to carry out measurements (Lavis and Milligan 1985).

However, the most fundamental worry about the epistemic approach is that it fails to realise the fundamental aim of SM, namely to explain how and why processes in nature take place because these processes cannot possibly depend on what we know about them. Surely, so the argument goes, the boiling of kettles or the spreading of gases has something to do with how the molecules constituting these systems behave and not with what we happen (or fail) to know about them (Redhead 1995; Albert 2000; Loewer 2001).[73]

4.9 The Relation between GSM and BSM

We began by saying that SM was the third pillar of modern physics. We then divided theoretical approaches in SM into two broad families, BSM and GSM. But is this not curious? How can it be that a fundamental theory in physics is divided into two approaches? The copresence of two different approaches would not by itself be a cause for concern if it were the case that the two formalisms were equivalent, or at least somehow inter-translatable (as, for instance, the Schrödinger and the Heisenberg picture in quantum mechanics). Unfortunately, they are not. As we have seen, the theoretical machineries of the two approaches are fundamentally different: they offer distinct descriptions of the same physical system and there is no obvious way to translate one into the other.

The situation is made worse by the fact that the theories usually serve different purposes. GSM is the workhorse of the practitioner. It provides the tools and methods to carry out a wide range of equilibrium calculations, which is why physicists often regard it as *the* formalism of statistical mechanics. Two examples illustrate this. In his textbook on SM, Isihara (1971) introduces the Gibbs formalism in a chapter called 'principles of statistical mechanics' and the first chapter of Landau and Lifshitz's (1980) canonical introduction, entitled 'the fundamental principles of statistical physics', is dedicated entirely to a discussion of the Gibbs formalism. However, as Lavis (2005, 246) notes, when confronted with the question of 'what is actually going on' in

---

[73] For further discussions of the epistemic approach, see Anta (2021), Shenker (2020), and Uffink (2011).

a physical system, physicists are often quick to desert GSM and offer an account of 'why SM works' in terms of BSM because, as we have seen, GSM has a number of features that jar with foundational accounts. And discrepancies are not restricted to foundational issues. In non-equilibrium situations, BSM is usually the theory of choice because, despite many attempts to extend GSM to non-equilibrium, no workable Gibbsian non-equilibrium theory has emerged yet.[74] But how can one use one formalism to explain the non-equilibrium behaviour of physical systems and to give a foundational account of SM, while continuing to use the other formalism for everyday equilibrium calculations?

There have been attempts to downplay the tension between BSM and GSM by arguing that the two formalisms end up producing the same predictions, at least as far as equilibrium calculations are concerned, and that discrepancies concerning foundational issues is something that we can live with.[75] While it is true that Boltzmannian and Gibbsian calculations agree in some cases, this agreement is not universal. There are cases in which GSM and BSM either make conflicting predictions about properties of a system or GSM remains silent.[76] Hence, the two formalisms not only differ in their theoretical characterisation of physical situations; they are also not empirically equivalent. This forecloses the escape route of non-committal pluralism, and any attempt to understand how SM works has to offer an account of the relation between BSM and GSM.

Somewhat surprisingly, the problem of the status of one theory vis-à-vis the other is a rather understudied issue, and among the few authors who discuss the issue there is no agreement on the matter. Lavis (2005) proposes a reconciliation of the two frameworks through giving up on the binary property of the system being or not being in equilibrium, which he replaces by the continuous property of *commonness*. Wallace (2020) argues that GSM is a more general framework in which the Boltzmannian approach may be understood as a special case.

Our own preferred suggestion is to regard BSM as a fundamental theory and GSM as an effective theory that offers a means to calculate values defined in BSM (Frigg and Werndl 2019; Werndl and Frigg 2020a). As Wells points out (2012), effective theories are ones that describe phenomena in a way that lends itself to effective computation. Effective theories can do this because they

---

[74] See Frigg (2008b), Sklar (1993), and Uffink (2007) for reviews.
[75] See, for instance, Davey (2009), Goldstein (2019), Goldstein, Lebowitz, Tumulka, and Zanghì (2020), and Wallace (2015).
[76] See Werndl and Frigg (2017b, 2020b).

are incomplete and leave out what is irrelevant for the purpose at hand. As a consequence, effective theories have a certain domain of application, and ideally it is known what this domain is. Understanding a theory as an effective theory has the advantage that foundational questions need not be asked about it because they pertain to the fundamental theory. In GSM, equilibrium is an ensemble property, and (as we note in the next section) the central notions of entropy and temperature are not definable in terms of functions on the state space X of a system. If we also take into account that there is no uncontroversial non-equilibrium theory, then the suggestion to regard GSM as an effective theory to calculate equilibrium values that are defined in GSM seems worth exploring. To this end we regard equilibrium values to be defined in BSM and show that these values are reproduced by GSM under certain conditions.

We have identified three conditions (which are subjects of three theorems), which all provide sufficient (but not necessary) conditions for phase averages, as calculated in GSM, to agree with the equilibrium values that come from BSM. Let us briefly state these three conditions.[77] The Khinchin Condition ensures that the fluctuations of the macro-variable f away from the phase average $\langle f \rangle$ are very small. In this case nearly all of the state space is taken up by a Boltzmannian equilibrium macro-region in which the Boltzmannian equilibrium macro-value is approximately equal to $\langle f \rangle$, and hence it is not surprising that the phase average is approximately equal to the Boltzmannian equilibrium value. The second condition is the Average Equivalence Condition. Here the crucial assumptions are that the macro-variable is a sum of a variable on the one-component space, that the macro-variable on the one-component space corresponds to a partition with cells of equal probability, and that the measure on state space is the product measure of the measure on the one-component space. If these conditions are satisfied, the Gibbsian phase averages agree with the Boltzmannian equilibrium values. The third condition is the Cancelling Out Condition: If the state space is divided up in such a way that next to the largest macro-region (which corresponds to the Boltzmannian equilibrium) there are always two macro-states of equal size whose average equals the Boltzmannian equilibrium value, then the Boltzmannian equilibrium value is equal to the value obtained by Gibbsian phase averaging. These three conditions are not always satisfied, and phase averages can differ from the Boltzmannian equilibrium values. There is an interesting open question about further characterisations of situations in which they agree, and about recognising situations in which they fail to do so.

---

[77] The Khinchin Condition is widely discussed; see, for instance, Lavis (2005). The other two conditions originate in Werndl and Frigg (2020b).

4.10 Open Questions for GSM

As has become clear in our discussion, GSM faces challenges as regards the interpretation of the theory once the reliance on the ensembles is renounced, and there remains a question of how to understand the approach to equilibrium from the perspective of GSM. A further question concerns the idea that SM ought to provide a reductive explanation of thermodynamics. As we have seen, equilibrium is a property of a probability distribution (and in Gibbs' interpretation, of an ensemble), which stands in an uneasy relation with an understanding of SM as a theory of individual systems. While this could be dismissed as a problem of interpretation, the same cannot be said about other issues. Chief among them is GSM's treatment of entropy and temperature. As we have seen in Section 4.1, the Gibbs entropy S_G is defined through the integral over $\rho_t(x)\log[\rho_t(x)]$, and there is no function s on X such that $S_G = \langle s(x) \rangle$. This means that the Gibbs entropy is undefinable in terms of the mechanical state of system. And the same goes for temperature, which is introduced by associating it with a term that plays the same functional role in a fundamental equation of GSM as temperature plays in a fundamental equation of thermodynamics (for a discussion, see Uffink 2007–96). What implications does this have for a putative reduction of TD to SM? Gibbs himself circumvents this issue by making no claim about reduction and instead discussing the relation between GSM and thermodynamics in terms of what he calls 'thermodynamic analogies' (Gibbs 1902/1981, ch. XIV). Hence, what a reduction of thermodynamics to GSM would look like is a question that deserves further exploration.

References

Adriaans, P. (2020). Information. In E. N. Zalta & U. Nodelman (Eds.), *The Stanford Encyclopedia of Philosophy*. https://plato.stanford.edu/archives/fall2020/entries/information.

Ainsworth, P. M. (2005). The spin-echo experiment and statistical mechanics. *Foundations of Physics Letters, 18* (7), 621–35.

Albert, D. Z. (2000). *Time and Chance*. Cambridge, MA: Harvard University Press.

Albert, D. Z. (2015). *After Physics*. Cambridge, MA: Harvard University Press.

Anta, J. (2021). Ignorance, milk and coffee: can epistemic states be causally-explanatorily relevant in statistical mechanics? *Foundations of Science, 28*(2), 489–505.

Argyris, J., Faust, G., & Haase, M. (1994). *An Exploration of Chaos: An Introduction for Natural Scientists and Engineers*. Amsterdam: Elsevier.

Arnold, V. I., & Avez, A. (1968). *Ergodic Problems of Classical Mechanics*. New York and Amsterdam: W. A. Benjamin.

Badino, M. (2020). Reassessing typicality explanations in statistical mechanics. In V. Allori (Ed.), *Statistical Mechanics and Scientific Explanation: Determinism, Indeterminism and Laws of Nature* (pp. 147–72). Singapore: World Scientific.

Baras, D., & Shenker, O. (2020). Calling for explanation: the case of the thermodynamic past state. *European Journal for Philosophy of Science, 10* (3), 1–20.

Batterman, R. W. (2002). *The Devil in the Details: Asymptotic Reasoning in Explanation, Reduction, and Emergence*. Oxford: Oxford University Press.

Berkovitz, J., Frigg, R., & Kronz, F. (2011). The ergodic hierarchy. In E. N. Zalta & U. Nodelman (Eds.), *The Stanford Encyclopedia of Philosophy*. https://plato.stanford.edu/entries/ergodic-hierarchy.

Blatt, J. M. (1959). An alternative approach to the ergodic problem. *Progress in Theoretical Physics, 22*(6), 745–55.

Boltzmann, L. (1877). Über die Beziehung zwischen dem zweiten Hauptsatze der mechanischen Wärmetheorie und der Wahrscheinlichkeitsrechnung resp. den Sätzen über das Wärmegleichgewicht. *Wiener Berichte, 76*, 373–435. Reprinted in F. Hasenöhrl (ed.), *Wissenschaftliche Abhandlungen*, Leipzig: J. A. Barth 1909, vol. 1902, pp. 1164–223.

Bricmont, J. (2001). Bayes, Boltzmann, and Bohm: probabilities in physics. In J. Bricmont, G. Ghirardi, & D. Dürr et al. (Eds.), *Chance in Physics Foundations and Perspectives* (Lecture Notes in Physics). Berlin: Springer.

Bricmont, J. (2022). *Making Sense of Statistical Mechanics*. Cham: Springer.

Brown, H. R., & Uffink, J. (2001). The origin of time-asymmetry in thermodynamics: the minus first law. *Studies in History and Philosophy of Modern Physics*, *32*(4), 525–38.

Brush, S. G. (1976). *The Kind of Motion We Call Heat*. Amsterdam: North Holland Publishing.

Butterfield, J. (2011a). Emergence, reduction and supervenience: a varied landscape. *Foundations of Physics*, *41*(6), 920–59.

Butterfield, J. (2011b). Less is different: emergence and reduction reconciled. *Foundations of Physics*, *41*(6), 1065–135.

Callender, C. (2004). There is no puzzle about the low-entropy past. In C. Hitchcock (Ed.), *Contemporary Debates in Philosophy of Science* (pp. 240–55). Malden, MA: Blackwell.

Cartwright, N. (1999). *The Dappled World: A Study of the Boundaries of Science*. Cambridge: Cambridge University Press.

Cercignani, C. (1998). *Ludwig Boltzmann: The Man Who Trusted Atoms*. Oxford: Oxford University Press.

Chandler, D. (1987). *Introduction to Modern Statistical Mechanics*. Oxford: Oxford University Press.

Chen, E. K. (2023). The past hypothesis and the nature of physical laws. In B. Loewer, E. Winsberg, & B. Weslake (Eds.), *Time's Arrows and the Probability Structure of the World* (pp. 204–248). Cambridge, MA: Harvard University Press.

Cornfeld, I. P., Fomin, S. V., & Sinai, Y. G. (1982). *Ergodic Theory*. Berlin: Springer.

Darrigol, O. (2018). *Atoms, Mechanics, and Probability: Ludwig Boltzmann's Statistico-Mechanical Writings – An Exegesis*. Oxford: Oxford University Press.

Darrigol, O. (2021). Boltzmann's reply to the Loschmidt paradox: a commented translation. *The European Physical Journal H*, *46*(1), Article 29.

Davey, K. (2008). The justification of probability measures in statistical mechanics. *Philosophy of Science*, *75*(1), 28–44.

Davey, K. (2009). What is Gibbs's canonical distribution? *Philosophy of Science*, *76*(5), 970–83.

Davies, P. (1974). *The Physics of Time Asymmetry*. Berkeley: University of California Press.

Dizadji-Bahmani, F. (2011). The Aharonov approach to equilibrium. *Philosophy of Science, 78*(5), 976–88.

Earman, J. (1986). *A Primer on Determinism.* Dordrecht: Reidel.

Earman, J. (2006). The past hypothesis: not even false. *Studies in History and Philosophy of Modern Physics, 37*(3), 399–430.

Earman, J., & Rédei, M. (1996). Why ergodic theory does not explain the success of equilibrium statistical mechanics. *The British Journal for Philosophy of Science, 47*(1), 63–78.

Ehrenfest, P., & Ehrenfest-Afanassjewa, T. (1912/1959). *The Conceptual Foundations of the Statistical Approach in Mechanics.* Ithaca, NY: Cornell University Press.

Emch, G. G. (2007). Quantum statistical physics. In J. Butterfield & J. Earman (Eds.), *Philosophy of Physics* (pp. 1075–182). Amsterdam: North Holland.

Farquhar, I. E. (1964). *Ergodic Theory in Statistical Mechanics.* New York: Interscience Publishers.

Farr, M. (2022). What's so special about initial conditions? Understanding the past hypothesis in directionless time. In Y. Ben-Menahem (Ed.), *Rethinking the Concept of Law of Nature: Natural Order in the Light of Contemporary Science* (pp. 205–24). Cham: Springer.

Feynman, R. P. (1965). *The Character of Physical Law.* Cambridge, MA: Massachusetts Institute of Technology Press.

Fine, T. (1973). *Theories of Probability: An Examination of Foundations.* New York: Academic Press.

Frigg, R. (2008a). Chance in Boltzmannian statistical mechanics. *Philosophy of Science, 75*(5), 670–81.

Frigg, R. (2008b). A field guide to recent work on the foundations of statistical mechanics. In D. Rickles (Ed.), *The Ashgate Companion to Contemporary Philosophy of Physics* (pp. 99–196). London: Ashgate.

Frigg, R. (2009). Typicality and the approach to equilibrium in Boltzmannian statistical mechanics. *Philosophy of Science, 76*(5), 997–1008.

Frigg, R. (2010). Probability in Boltzmannian statistical mechanics. In G. Ernst & A. Hüttemann (Eds.), *Time, Chance and Reduction: Philosophical Aspects of Statistical Mechanics* (pp. 92–118). Cambridge: Cambridge University Press.

Frigg, R. (2011). Why typicality does not explain the approach to equilibrium. In M. Suárez (Ed.), *Probabilities, Causes and Propensities in Physics* (pp. 77–93, Synthese Library). Dordrecht: Springer.

Frigg, R. (2016). Chance and determinism. In A. Hájek & C. Hitchcock (Eds.), *The Oxford Handbook of Probability and Philosophy* (pp. 460–74). Oxford: Oxford University Press.

Frigg, R., & Hoefer, C. (2015). The best Humean system for statistical mechanics. *Erkenntnis, 80*(3), 551–74.

Frigg, R., & Werndl, C. (2011). Explaining thermodynamic-like behavior in terms of epsilon-ergodicity. *Philosophy of Science, 78*(3), 628–52.

Frigg, R., & Werndl, C. (2012). Demystifying typicality. *Philosophy of Science, 79*(5), 917–29.

Frigg, R., & Werndl, C. (2019). Statistical mechanics: a tale of two theories. *The Monist, 102,* 424–38.

Frigg, R., & Werndl, C. (2021). Can somebody please say what Gibbsian statistical mechanics says? *The British Journal for Philosophy of Science, 72*(1), 105–29.

Frigg, R., & Werndl, C. (2023). Boltzmannian non-equilibrium and local variables. In C. Soto (Ed.), *Current Debates in Philosophy of Science: In Honor of Roberto Torretti* (pp. 275–287). Cham: Springer.

Frisch, M. (2011). From Arbuthnot to Boltzmann: the past hypothesis, the best system, and the special sciences. *Philosophy of Science, 78*(5), 1001–11.

Galavotti, M. C. (2005). *Philosophical Introduction to Probability.* Stanford, CA: CSLI Publications.

Gibbs, J. W. (1902/1981). *Elementary Principles in Statistical Mechanics.* Woodbridge: Oxbow Press.

Gillies, D. (2000). *Philosophical Theories of Probability.* London: Routledge.

Goldstein, S. (2001). Boltzmann's approach to statistical mechanics. In J. Bricmont, G. Ghirardi, D. Dürr et al. (Eds.), *Chance in Physics. Foundations and Perspectives* (pp. 39–54). Berlin: Springer.

Goldstein, S. (2019). Individualist and ensemblist approaches to the foundations of statistical mechanics. *The Monist, 102,* 439–57.

Goldstein, S., Lebowitz, J. L., Tumulka, R., & Zanghì, N. (2020). Gibbs and Boltzmann entropy in classical and quantum mechanics. In V. Allori (Ed.), *Statistical Mechanics and Scientific Explanation: Determinism, Indeterminism and Laws of Nature* (pp. 519–81). Singapore: World Scientific.

Hahn, E. L. (1950). Spin echoes. *Physics Review, 80,* 580–94.

Hájek, A. (2019). Interpretations of Probability. In E. N. Zalta, & U. Nodelman (Eds.), *The Stanford Encyclopedia of Philosophy.* https://plato.stanford.edu/archives/fall2019/entries/probability-interpret.

Hand, D. J. (2008). *Statistics: A Very Short Introduction.* Oxford: Oxford University Press.

Hemmo, M., & Shenker, O. (2022). Is the Mentaculus the best system of our world? In Y. Ben-Menahem (Ed.), *Rethinking the Concept of Law of Nature: Natural Order in the Light of Contemporary Science* (pp. 89–128). Cham: Springer.

Hill, T. L. (1956/1987). *Statistical Mechanics: Principles and Selected Applications*. Mineola, NY: Dover.

Hoefer, C. (2019). *Chance in the World: A Humean Guide to Objective Chance* (Oxford Studies in Philosophy of Science). New York: Oxford University Press.

Howson, C., & Urbach, P. (2006). *Scientific Reasoning: The Bayesian Approach* (3rd ed.). Chicago and La Salle: Open Court.

Isihara, A. (1971). *Statistical Physics*. London: Academic Press.

Jaynes, E. T. (1983). *Papers on Probability, Statistics, and Statistical Physics*. Dordrecht: Reidl.

Jebeile, J. (2020). The Kac ring or the art of making idealisations. *Foundations of Physics*, *50*(10), 1152–70.

Katok, A., & Hasselblatt, B. (1995). *Introduction to the Modern Theory of Dynamical Systems*. Cambridge: Cambridge University Press.

Khinchin, A. I. (1949/1960). *Mathematical Foundations of Statistical Mechanics*. Mineola, NY: Dover Publications.

Kittel, C. (1958/2004). *Elementary Statistical Physics*. Mineola, NY: Dover Publications.

Landau, L. D., & Lifshitz, E. M. (1980). *Statistical Physics: Part 1* (3rd ed.). Oxford: Pergamon.

Lavis, D. (2004). The spin-echo system reconsidered. *Foundations of Physics*, *34*, 245–73.

Lavis, D. (2005). Boltzmann and Gibbs: An attempted reconciliation. *Studies in History and Philosophy of Modern Physics*, *36*, 245–73.

Lavis, D., Kühn, R., & Frigg, R. (2021). Becoming large, becoming infinite. The anatomy of thermal physics and phase transitions in finite systems. *Foundations of Physics*, *51*, 1–69.

Lavis, D., & Milligan, P. (1985). Essay review of Jaynes' collected papers. *The British Journal for Philosophy of Science*, *36*, 193–210.

Lavis, D. A. (2008). Boltzmann, Gibbs, and the concept of equilibrium. *Philosophy of Science*, *75*, 682–96.

Lavis, D. A. (2015). *Equilibrium Statistical Mechanics of Lattice Models*. Cham: Springer.

Lebowitz, J. L. (1993). Macroscopic laws, microscopic dynamics, time's arrow and Boltzmann's entropy. *Physica A*, *194*, 1–27.

Leeds, S. (1989). Malament and Zabell on Gibbs phase averaging. *Philosophy of Science*, *56*, 325–40.

Lewis, D. K. (1986). A subjectivist's guide to objective chance. In *Philosophical Papers* (pp. 83–132). Oxford: Oxford University Press.

Linden, N., Popesu, S., Short, A. J., & Andreas, W. (2009). Quantum mechanical evolution towards thermal equilibrium. *Physical Review E, 79*, Article 061103.

Loewer, B. (2001). Determinism and chance. *Studies in History and Philosophy of Modern Physics, 32*, 609–29.

Loschmidt, J. J. (1876). Über die Zustand des Wärmegleichgewichtes eines Systems von Körpern mit Rücksicht auf die Schwerkraft. *Wiener Berichte, 73*, 128–42.

Lyon, A. (2016). Kolmogorov's axiomatisation and its discontents. In A. Hájek & C. Hitchcock (Eds.), *The Oxford Handbook of Probability and Philosophy* (pp. 155–66).

Malament, D. B., & Zabell, S. L. (1980). Why Gibbs phase averages work. *Philosophy of Science, 47*, 339–49.

Maudlin, T. (2020). The Grammar of Typicality. In V. Allori (Ed.), *Statistical Mechanics and Scientific Explanation. Determinism, Indeterminism and Laws of Nature* (pp. 231–51). Singapore: World Scientific.

Maxwell, J. C. (1860/1965). Illustrations of the Dynamical Theory of Gases. In W. D. Niven (Ed.), *The Scientific Papers of James Clerk Maxwell* (pp. 377–409). New York: Dover Publications.

McCoy, C. D. (2020). An Alternative Interpretation of Statistical Mechanics. *Erkenntnis*(85), 1–21.

McLaughlin, B., & Bennett, K. (2021). Supervenience. In E. N. Zalta & U. Nodelman (Eds.), *The Stanford Encyclopedia of Philosophy*. https://plato.stanford.edu/archives/sum2021/entries/supervenience.

Myrvold, W., Albert, D. Z., Callender, C., & Ismael, J. (2016). Book Symposium: David Albert, *After Physics*. *PhilSci Archive* http://philsci-archive.pitt.edu/12871.

Myrvold, W. C. (2016). Probabilities in statistical mechanics. In C. Hitchcock & A. Hájek (Eds.), *Oxford Handbook of Probability and Philosophy*. Oxford: Oxford University Press.

Myrvold, W. C. (2021). *Beyond Chance and Credence: A Theory of Hybrid Probabilities*. Oxford: Oxford University Press.

Palacios, P. (2022). *Emergence and Reduction in Physics* (Cambridge Elements). Cambridge: Cambridge University Press.

Parker, D. (2005). Thermodynamic irreversibility: does the big bang explain what it purports to explain? *Philosophy of Science, 72*(5), 751–63.

Pathria, R. K., & Beale, P. D. (2011). *Statistical Mechanics* (3rd ed.). Oxford: Academic Press.

Penrose, O. (1970). *Foundations of Statistical Mechanics: A Deductive Treatment* (Oxford). Pergamon Press.

Penrose, R. (2006). *The Road to Reality: A Complete Guide to the Laws of the Universe*. London: Vintage.

Petersen, K. (1983). *Ergodic Theory*. Cambridge: Cambridge University Press.

Price, H. (2004). On the origins of the arrow of time: why there is still a puzzle about the low-entropy past. In C. Hitchcock (Ed.), *Contemporary Debates in Philosophy of Science* (pp. 219–39). Malden, MA: Blackwell.

Rédei, M. (1992). Krylov's proof that statistical mechanics cannot be founded on classical mechanics and interpretation of classical statistical mechanical probabilities. *Philosophia Naturalis, 29*, 268–84.

Redhead, M. L. G. (1995). *From Physics to Metaphysics*. Cambridge: Cambridge University Press.

Reiss, H. (1965). *Methods of Thermodynamics*. New York: Blaisdell Publishing Company.

Ridderbos, K. (2002). The coarse-graining approach to statistical mechanics: How blissful is our ignorance? *Studies in History and Philosophy of Modern Physics, 33*, 65–77.

Ridderbos, T. M., & Redhead, M. L. G. (1998). The spin-echo experiments and the second law of thermodynamics. *Foundations of Physics, 28*, 1237–70.

Roberts, B. W. (2022). *Reversing the Arrow of Time*. Cambridge: Cambridge University Press.

Robertson, K. (2020). Asymmetry, abstraction and autonomy: justifying coarse-graining in statistical mechanics. *The British Journal for the Philosophy of Science, 71*(2), 547–79.

Schrödinger, E. (1952/1989). *Statistical Thermodynamics*. Mineola, NY: Dover.

Shenker, O. (2017a). Foundation of statistical mechanics: mechanics by itself. *Philosophy Compass, 12*(12), e12465.

Shenker, O. (2017b). Foundation of statistical mechanics: the auxiliary hypotheses. *Philosophy Compass, 12*(12), e12464.

Shenker, O. (2020). Information vs. entropy vs. probability. *European Journal for Philosophy of Science, 10*, Article No 5.

Sklar, L. (1993). *Physics and Chance: Philosophical Issues in the Foundations of Statistical Mechanics*. Cambridge: Cambridge University Press.

te Vrug, M., Tóth, G. I., & Wittkowski, R. (2021). Master equations for Wigner functions with spontaneous collapse and their relation to thermodynamic irreversibility. *Journal of Computational Electronics, 20*, 2209–31.

Tolman, R. C. (1938/1979). *The Principles of Statistical Mechanics*. Mineola, NY: Dover.

Uffink, J. (1995). Can the maximum entropy principle be explained as a consistency requirement? *Studies in History and Philosophy of Modern Physics, 26*, 223–61.

Uffink, J. (1996a). The constraint rule of the maximum entropy principle. *Studies in History and Philosophy of Modern Physics, 27*, 47–79.

Uffink, J. (1996b). Nought but molecules in motion (review essay of Lawrence Sklar: *Physics and Chance*). *Studies in History and Philosophy of Modern Physics, 27*, 373–87.

Uffink, J. (2001). Bluff your way in the second law of thermodynamics. *Studies in History and Philosophy of Modern Physics, 32*, 305–94.

Uffink, J. (2007). Compendium of the foundations of classical statistical physics. In J. Butterfield & J. Earman (Eds.), *Philosophy of Physics* (pp. 923–1047).

Uffink, J. (2011). Subjective probability and statistical physics. In C. Beisbart & S. Hartmann (Eds.), *Probabilities in Physics* (pp. 25–49). Oxford: Oxford University Press.

Uffink, J. (2022). Boltzmann's Work in Statistical Physics. In E. N. Zalta & U. Nodelman (Eds.), *The Stanford Encyclopedia of Philosophy*. https://plato.stanford.edu/archives/sum2022/entries/statphys-Boltzmann.

van Lith, J. (2001). Ergodic theory, interpretations of probability and the foundations of statistical mechanics. *Studies in History and Philosophy of Modern Physics, 32*, 581–94.

von Plato, J. (1988). Ergodic theory and the foundations of probability. In B. Skyrms & W. W. Harper (Eds.), *Causation, Chance and Credence* (pp. 257–77). Dordrecht: Kluwer.

von Plato, J. (1989). Probability in dynamical systems. In J. E. Fenstad, I. T. Frolov, & R. Hilpinen (Eds.), *Logic, Methodology and Philosophy of Science, Vol. VIII* (pp. 427–43). Amsterdam: North-Holland.

Vranas, P. B. M. (1998). Epsilon-ergodicity and the success of equilibrium statistical mechanics. *Philosophy of Science, 65*, 688–708.

Wallace, D. (2015). The quantitative content of statistical mechanics. *Studies in History and Philosophy of Science Part B: Studies in History and Philosophy of Modern Physics, 52*, 285–93.

Wallace, D. (2020). The necessity of Gibbsian statistical mechanics. In V. Allori (Ed.), *Statistical Mechanics and Scientific Explanation. Determinism, Indeterminism and Laws of Nature* (pp. 583–616). World Scientific.

Wells, J. D. (2012). *Effective Theories in Physics: From Planetary Orbits to Elementary Particle Masses*. Heidelberg: Springer.

Werndl, C. (2013). Justifying typicality measures of Boltzmannian statistical mechanics and dynamical systems. *Studies in History and Philosophy of Modern Physics, 44*(4), 470–9.

Werndl, C., & Frigg, R. (2015a). Reconceptualising equilibrium in Boltzmannian statistical mechanics and characterising its existence. *Studies in History and Philosophy of Modern Physics, 49*(1), 19–31.

Werndl, C., & Frigg, R. (2015b). Rethinking Boltzmannian equilibrium. *Philosophy of Science, 82*(5), 1224–35.

Werndl, C., & Frigg, R. (2017a). Boltzmannian equilibrium in stochastic systems. In M. Massimi & J.-W. Romeijn (Eds.), *Proceedings of the EPSA15 Conference* (pp. 243–54). Berlin: Springer.

Werndl, C., & Frigg, R. (2017b). Mind the gap: Boltzmannian vs Gibbsian equilibrium. *Philosophy of Science, 84*, 1289–1302.

Werndl, C., & Frigg, R. (2020a). Taming abundance: on the relation between Boltzmannian and Gibbsian statistical mechanics. In V. Allori (Ed.), *Statistical Mechanics and Scientific Explanation: Determinism, Indeterminism and Laws of Nature* (pp. 617–46). World Scientific.

Werndl, C., & Frigg, R. (2020b). When do Gibbsian phase averages and Boltzmannian equilibrium values agree? *Studies in History and Philosophy of Modern Physics, 72*, 46–69.

Werndl, C., & Frigg, R. (2023). When does a Boltzmannian equilibrium exist? In C. Soto (Ed.), *Current Debates in Philosophy of Science: In Honor of Roberto Torretti* (pp. forthcoming). Cham: Springer.

Wilhelm, I. (2022). Typical: a theory of typicality and typicality explanation. *The British Journal for the Philosophy of Science, 73*(2), 561–81.

Williamson, J. (2010). *In Defence of Objective Bayesianism.* Oxford: Oxford University Press.

Winsberg, E. (2004a). Can conditioning on the 'past hypothesis' militate against the reversibility objection? *Philosophy of Science, 71*, 489–504.

Winsberg, E. (2004b). Laws and statistical mechanics. *Philosophy of Science, 71*, 707–18.

Zanghì, N. (2005). I Fondamenti concettuali dell'approccio statistico in Fisica. In V. Allori, M. Dorato, F. Laudisa, & N. Zanghì (Eds.), *La Natura Delle Cose: Introduzione ai Fundamenti e alla Filosofia della Fisica* (pp. 139–227). Roma: Carocci.

Zermelo, E. (1896). Über einen Satz der Dynamik und die mechanische Wärmetheorie. *Annalen der Physik, 57*, 485–94.

Acknowledgements

Authors are listed in alphabetical order; the work is fully collaborative. We would like to thank David Lavis, Patricia Palacios, Jos Uffink, Giovanni Valente, and David Wallace for helpful discussions on the subject matter of this Element. We are also grateful to two anonymous referees for providing extensive comments on the manuscript. And last but not least, we would like to thank Jim Weatherall for inviting us to participate in this series, and for all his counsel on the long way from a rough idea to complete manuscript.

Cambridge Elements ≡

The Philosophy of Physics

James Owen Weatherall
University of California, Irvine

James Owen Weatherall is Professor of Logic and Philosophy of Science at the University of California, Irvine. He is the author, with Cailin O'Connor, of *The Misinformation Age: How False Beliefs Spread* (Yale, 2019), which was selected as a *New York Times* Editors' Choice and Recommended Reading by *Scientific American*. His previous books were *Void: The Strange Physics of Nothing* (Yale, 2016) and the *New York Times* bestseller *The Physics of Wall Street: A Brief History of Predicting the Unpredictable* (Houghton Mifflin Harcourt, 2013). He has published approximately fifty peer-reviewed research articles in journals in leading physics and philosophy of science journals and has delivered over 100 invited academic talks and public lectures.

About the Series

This Cambridge Elements series provides concise and structured introductions to all the central topics in the philosophy of physics. The Elements in the series are written by distinguished senior scholars and bright junior scholars with relevant expertise, producing balanced, comprehensive coverage of multiple perspectives in the philosophy of physics.

Cambridge Elements ☰

The Philosophy of Physics

Printed in the United States
by Baker & Taylor Publisher Services